BAG DESIGN

A HANDBOOK FOR
ACCESSORIES DESIGNERS

FASHIONARY

FASHIONARY

Edited by Mini Miss Mia & Penter Yip
Illustration by Sarah Chow and Mini Miss Mia
Copy editing & proofreading by Ginny Chan

Credit to the contributors of this project:
Vikki Yau, Zoe Kwok, Jessie Yeung, Mountain Yam,
Karmuel Young, Charlene Wong, Sam Ho

ISBN 978-988-77108-0-6
SN FPV111611PBCB

Designed and published by Fashionary International Ltd
Manufactured in China

Bag Design is an ongoing project. If you have any feedback,
please don't hesitate to send it to
feedback@fashionary.org

🄵 @ fashionary
🐦 @ fashionarybook
🄸 @ fashionary
🄿 @ fashionary

Fashionary Team
Nov 2016

CONTENTS

BAGS & SMALL LEATHER GOODS

CLUTCH & HANDHELD BAGS

Pouch
(refer to P. 60)

Clutch
(refer to P. 61)

Envelope Clutch
(refer to P. 62)

Box Clutch

Minaudière
(refer to P. 63)

Kiss Lock Clutch
(refer to P. 64)

Bracelet Bag

Wristlet
(refer to P. 65)

Bermuda Bag

Basket

Knot Bag

Pochette

Hat Box

Box Bag
(refer to P. 66)

Doctor's Bag
(refer to P. 67)

Boston Bag
(refer to P. 68)

Gladstone Bag
(refer to P. 69)

Handheld Handbag
(refer to P. 70-75)

CROSSBODY & SHOULDER BAGS

Baguette Bag
(refer to P. 76)

Hobo Bag
(refer to P. 77)

Straw Bag / Beach Bag /
Kenya Bag
(refer to P. 78)

Muff Bag

Shopper Bag / Tote Bag
(refer to P. 79-80)

Shopper Bag / Tote Bag
(refer to P. 81-82)

Woven Tote

Fringe Bag
(refer to P. 83)

Bucket Bag
(refer to P. 84)

Squaw Bag

Accordion Handbag
(refer to P. 85)

Canteen Bag
(refer to P. 86)

Saddle Bag
(refer to P. 87-88)

Satchel
(refer to P. 89)

Quilted Sling /
Crossbody Bag
(refer to P. 90)

Lady Camera Bag
(refer to P. 91)

One Strap Bookbag /
One Shoulder Backpack /
Sling Backpack
(refer to P. 92)

Haversack

BACKPACKS & WAIST BAGS

Belt Bag
(refer to P. 93)

Waist Pack / Bum Bag
(refer to P. 94)

Sports Waist Belt Bag

Day Pack
(refer to P. 95)

Backpack
(refer to P. 96)

Drawstring Backpack

BACKPACKS & WAIST BAGS (CONT'D)

Randoseru

Knapsack
(refer to P. 98)

Army Duffel Bag

School Bag
a small backpack, suitable for
a one-day hike or for carrying
books around campus

Rucksack
(refer to P. 99)

Satchel Backpack
(refer to P. 100)

ATHLETIC & FUNCTIONAL BAGS

Security Pouch /
Small Traveling Pouch
(refer to P. 101)

Wash Bag / Cosmetic Bag
(refer to P. 102)

Dopp Kit

Weekender
(refer to P. 103)

Sports Duffel Bag
(refer to P. 104)

Barrel Bag / Holdall
(refer to P. 105)

Bowling Bag
(refer to P. 106-107)

Safari Bag
always made of canvas fabrics

Messenger Bag /
Courier Bag
(refer to P. 108)

Field Bag
(refer to P. 109)

Battle Bag

Computer Bag / Laptop Bag
(refer to P. 110)

Trunk Bag
placed at the back of motorcycles

Saddle / Pannier Bag
a bag carried in pairs attached to the
sides of a bicycle or motorcycle

Camera Bag
(refer to P. 111)

Lens Bag

Diaper Bag

Packing Cubes

Tennis Bag

Hiking Backpack
(refer to P. 112)

Golf Bag
(refer to P. 113)

Gig Bag / Guitar Bag

Portfolio Bag

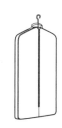
Garment Bag

TRUNKS & LUGGAGE

Briefcase

Suitcase

Attaché Case

Rigid Case

Cosmestic Case

Pilot Case

TRUNKS & LUGGAGE (CONT'D)

Camera Hard Case

Instrument Case
(e.g. French Horn Case)

Hardside Luggage
(refer to P. 114-115)

Softside Luggage
(refer to P. 116-117)

Trunk

Camp Trunk

WALLETS & PURSES

Purse

Coin Purse

Clasp Purse

Continental / Long Wallet
(refer to P. 118)

Zip-around Wallet
(refer to P. 119)

Credit Card Wallet

Bi-fold Wallet
(refer to P. 120)

Tri-fold Wallet

Wallet with Chain

Wallet with Strap

Travel / Passport Wallet

Phone Case Wallet

LEATHER BELTS

Cinch Belt

D-Ring Belt

Grommet Belt

Braided Leather Belt

Surcingle Belt
woven belt with leather tab
and metal buckle

Safari Belt

Western Belt

Cartridge Belt

Money Belt

Snake Belt

Sam Browne Belt

Kidney Belt

OTHER SMALL LEATHER GOODS

Key Case
(refer to P. 121)

Glasses Case

Glasses Pouch

Card Holder

Writing Case

Money Clip

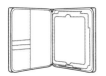
Tablet Case / Sleeve

Phone Case

Luggage Tag

Knife Sheath

Manicure Set Case

Pencil Case

HISTORICAL & FOLK BAGS

MEDIEVAL PERIOD (5ᵀᴴ - 15ᵀᴴ CENTURY)

Embroidered Purse
France
c. 1170-90

Pouch
France
c. 1200-1300

Purse
c. 1200-1300

Pouch
France
c. 1200-1300

Girdle & Almoner
England
c. 1300

Case for Enamel Diptych
England
c. 1300

Leather Pouch
England
c. 1300

Reliquary Bag
Rhineland
c. 1300

Escarcelle
England
c. 1300-1400

Gypsere
England
c. 1300-1400

Penner & Inkhorn
England
c. 1300-1400

Purse
Spain
c. 1400-1480

RENAISSANCE PERIOD (15ᵀᴴ - 17ᵀᴴ CENTURY)

Drawstring Pouch
England
c. 1500

Calthorpe Purse
England
c. 1540

Purse
Italy
c. 1550

Sweetmeat Purse
England
c. 1580-1600

Sweetmeat Purse
England
c. 1590

Purse
England
c. 1600

Purse
England
c. 1600

Purse
England
c. 1600

Sweetmeat Purse
England
c. 1600

Sweetmeat Purse
England
c. 1600

Gaming Bag
France
c. 1600

Tapestry Purse
France
c. 1600

Purse
England
c. 1600-50

Sweetmeat Purse
England
c. 1630-50

Drawstring Purse
England
c. 1634

Sweetmeat Purse
England
c. 1670

Sweetmeat Purse
France
c. 1670

Sweetmeat Purse
France
c. 1670

Letter Case
France
c. 1670

Sweetmeat Purse
France
c. 1670-80

Purse
England
c. 1680

Bridal Purse
France
c. 1680

Sweetmeat Purse
France
c. 1680-90

Bridal Purse
France
c. 1680-99

Tie-on Pocket
England
c. 1700

Letter Case
France
c. 1740-50

Sweetmeat Purse
England
c. 1750

Pocket Case
France
c. 1750

Pocket Case
England
c. 1750-75

Tie-on Pocket
England
c. 1760

Long Purse
England
late c. 1700

Knitted Silk Purse
with Finger Ring
England
late c. 1700

Reticule
England
c. 1800

Reticule
England
early c. 1800

Silk Bag
France
early c. 1800

Reticule
Europe
early c. 1800

Reticule
England
c. 1800-09

Tie-on Pocket
England
c. 1800-19

Miser's Purse
England
c. 1800-19

Miser's Purse
Europe
c. 1815-19

Purse
England
c. 1815-19

Purse
England
c. 1825-29

Drawstring Purse
England
c. 1825-29

Canvas Bag with Beads
England
c. 1830

Purse
France
c. 1830-49

Reticule
England
c. 1840-49

Miser's Purse
England
c. 1840-49

Miser's Purse
England
c. 1840-49

Bag
England
c. 1850

Bag
England
c. 1850-59

Reticule
England
c. 1850-59

Reticule
England
c. 1850-59

Reticule
England
c. 1850-59

Bag
England
c. 1850-59

Crocheted Coin Purse with
Perfume Bottle on Top
France
c. 1855

Reticule
India
c. 1860

Pocket
England
c. 1860-65

Card Case
Europe
c. 1860-65

Lingerie Bag
Germany
c. 1860-65

Lingerie Bag
Germany
c. 1860-65

Workbag
England
c. 1875-79

Metal Purse
England
c. 1880

Workbag
England
c. 1880

Velvet Bag
France
c. 1880

Leather Hand and
Wrist Bag
Germany
c. 1880

Leather Hand and
Wrist Bag
Germany
c. 1880

AGE OF ENLIGHTENMENT (17TH - 19TH CENTURY) (CONT'D)

Lingerie Bag
Germany
c. 1860-65

Jug-shaped Coin Purse
Germany
c. 1865

Handbag
France
c. 1860-69

Handbag with Telescope
England
c. 1870

Belt Bag
England / Germany
c. 1870

Chatelaine Purse
England
c. 1870-75

Gladstone Bag
Europe
c. 1880-85

Hunting Bag
Switzerland
c. 1890

Handbag
England
c. 1890

Handbag
England
c. 1890

Handbag
England
c. 1890

Gladstone Bag
Scotland
c. 1890

Chateline
Germany
c. 1890

Belt with Leather Bags
Germany
c. 1890

Chatelaine with
Notebook & Pencil
England
19th century

Chateline
England
19th century

Leather Chateline
France
19th century

Chatelaine with
Notebook & Pencil
Germany
19th century

FOLK AND TRADITIONAL BAGS FROM EAST TO WEST

Inro
Japan

Kinchaku
Japan

Yunnan Bag
China

Qing Belt Bag
China

Hebao / Purse in
Ru-Yi shape
China

Bokjumeoni /
Fortune Pouch
Korea

Bayong
Philippines

Jhola
India

Potli
India

Beads & Shell Bag
Africa

Dilly Bag
Australian

Woollen Çanta
Turkey

Medicine Bag
America

Kiowa Pipe Bag
America

Ojibwe Bandolier Bag
America

Métis Fire Bag
Canada

Sporran
Scotland

Dräktväskor
Sweden

SIGNATURE BAGS

DESIGNER SIGNATURE BAGS

Pashli
– 3.1 Phillip Lim

Pons Backpack
– Agneskovacs

De Manta Clutch
– Alexander McQueen

Knuckle Box Clutch
– Alexander McQueen

Marti
– Alexander Wang

Prisma
– Alexander Wang

Rocco
– Alexander Wang

Geo Bag
– Alviero Martini

I'm Not A Plastic Bag
– Anya Hindmarch

City
– Balenciaga

Veneta Bag
– Bottega Veneta

Classic Bucket Bag
– Building Block

Cylinder Sling Bag
– Building Block

Classic Box Bag
– Celine

Luggage Tote
– Celine

Trapeze
– Celine

Vertical Cabas Tote
– Celine

2.55
– Chanel

Boy
– Chanel

Classic Flap Bag
– Chanel

Drew
– Chloé

Faye
– Chloé

Marcie
– Chloé

Paraty
– Chloé

Sweet Charity Bag
– Christian Louboutin

Lady Dior / Princess Bag
– Christian Dior

Saddle Bag
– Christian Dior

Mini Bucket
– Coach

Priscillini
– Corto Moltedo

Miss Sicily
– Dolce & Gabbana

Baguette
– Fendi

Peekaboo
with Bag Bugs
– Fendi

Petite 2Jours
– Fendi

Kånken
– Fjällräven

Antigona
– Givenchy

Centenary
– Globe Trotter

Nightingale
– Givenchy

Pandora Box
– Givenchy

Saint Louis PM Tote
– Goyard

Jackie
– Gucci

Bamboo Classic Top
Handle
– Gucci

Soho Disco Bag
– Gucci

Speedy
– Gucci

Birkin
– Hermès

Kelly
– Hermès

Constance
– Hermès

Evelyne
– Hermès

Little America Backpack
– Herschel Supply Co.

Bao Bao
– Issey Miyake

Chandra Clutch
– Jimmy Choo

Pebble Leather Backpack
– Kara

K/Klassic
– Karl Lagerfeld

Cedar Street
– Kate Spade

Kalifornia Gommato Bag
– Kenzo

Alex Black Widow
– Les Petits Joueurs

Amazona
– Loewe

Puzzle
– Loewe

Flamenco Knot Bag
– Loewe

Le Pliage Tote
– Longchamp

Alma
– Louis Vuitton

Classic Neverfull
– Louis Vuitton

Pégase Légère 55
– Louis Vuitton

Speedy
– Louis Vuitton

Twist
– Louis Vuitton

Bucket Bag
– Mansur Gavriel

Classic Q Lil Ukita Bag
– Marc Jacobs

Pretty Nylon Tote
– Marc Jacobs

Stark Backpack
– MCM

Selma
– Michael Kors

Matelassé Leather Bag
– Miu Miu

Vitello Lux Bow Bag
– Miu Miu

Alexa
– Mulberry

Bayswater
– Mulberry

Lily
– Mulberry

Ballet
– Nina Ricci

Pan Am Bag
– Pan Am

Tanker
– Porter

Prada Backpack
– Prada

Tessuto Fiocco
– Prada

Tessuto Gaufre Tote
– Prada

PS1
– Proenza Schouler

Ricky
– Ralph Lauren

Leo Tote
– Rebecca Minkoff

Topsa
– Rimowa

Cabas Y Tote
– Saint Laurent

Classic Sac De Jour
– Saint Laurent

Classic Monogram
– Saint Laurent

Ginny
– Salvatore Ferragamo

Sofia
– Salvatore Ferragamo

Box Albion
– Sophie Hulme

The Correspondent
– Steamline Luggage

Falabella
– Stella Mccartney

Classic Satchel
– The Cambridge Satchel
Company

D Bag
– Tod's

Ella
– Tory Burch

Truss Woven Large Tote
– Truss

Vapor
– Tumi

My Rockstud
– Valentino

Rockstud Tote
– Valentino

Medusa
– Versace

Liberty Tote
– Victoria Beckham

Bombette
– Viktor & Rolf

AVANT-GARDE BAGS

Chanel Girl
– Chanel

Natural Arid Clutch
– Chiyome

Nile
– Côte & Ciel

Crane Bag
– Digest Design Workshop

Rae
– Finell

Harness Day Bag
– Fleet Ilya

Collapse Series
– Frrry

Artist Pallet
– Jacquemus

Glove Bag
– Jean Paul Gaultier

Lunch Bag
– Jil Sander

Pyramid
– Jil Sander

Cupcake
– Judith Leiber

Gift Box Bag
– Kate Spade

Boxed Clutch
– Kenzo

Petite Malle
– Louis Vuitton

Amor Fati
– M2Malletier

Arm Candy
– Maison Margiela

Biker Jacket Shoulder Bag
– Moschino

Baby Bow
– Niels Peeraer

Ice Cream Bag
– Nila Anthony

Tube of Lipstick Bag
– Nila Anthony

Mr & Mrs West,
A Love Story
– Olympia Le-Tan

Cherry Knuckleduster
Clutch
– Undercover

C'est Ahh... Shoulder Bag
– Yazbukey

BAG DETAILS

HANDLES & STRAPS

Top Handle / Flat Top Handle

Bamboo Handle

Cut-out Handle

Acrylic / Resin / Plastic Handle

Wooden Handle

Rope with Loop

Rope Handle with Loop Attachment

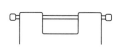

Scroll-in Handle

Knotted Handle

Loop Handle

Flat Handle

Handle with Ring and Round Tab

Handle with Ring and Square Tab

Adjustable Buckle Handle

Leather Handle with Clasp

Rolled Handle

Braided Leather Handle

Fendi Wide Strap

Crossbody Strap with Adjustable Buckle

Double Buckle Crossbody Strap

Beaded Handle

Metal Chain Strap

Leather-woven Chain Strap

Curb Chain Handle / Leather Handle with Chain

Tote Handle with Toggles

Woven Straps with Fringe Trim

Rope Handle

Two-Way Adjustable Crossbody and Shoulder Strap

Webbing Handle

Rattan Handle

CLOSURES

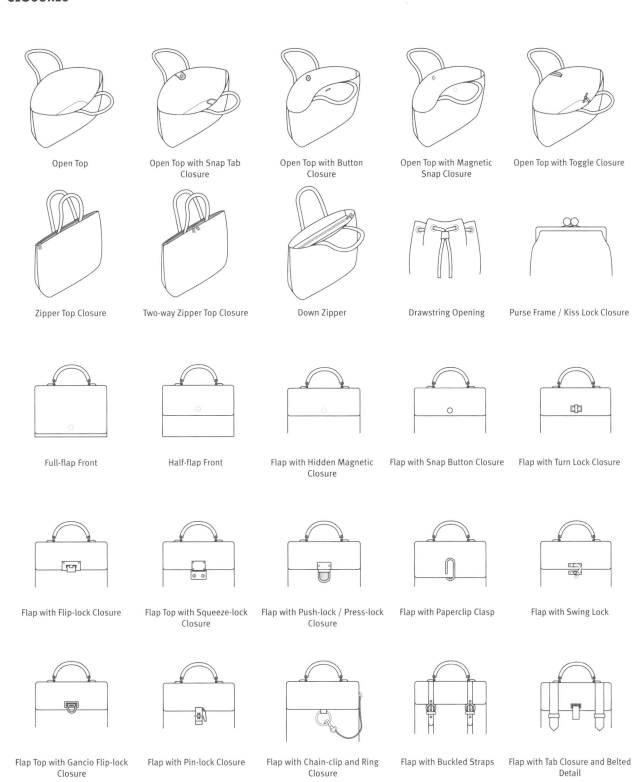

Open Top

Open Top with Snap Tab Closure

Open Top with Button Closure

Open Top with Magnetic Snap Closure

Open Top with Toggle Closure

Zipper Top Closure

Two-way Zipper Top Closure

Down Zipper

Drawstring Opening

Purse Frame / Kiss Lock Closure

Full-flap Front

Half-flap Front

Flap with Hidden Magnetic Closure

Flap with Snap Button Closure

Flap with Turn Lock Closure

Flap with Flip-lock Closure

Flap Top with Squeeze-lock Closure

Flap with Push-lock / Press-lock Closure

Flap with Paperclip Clasp

Flap with Swing Lock

Flap Top with Gancio Flip-lock Closure

Flap with Pin-lock Closure

Flap with Chain-clip and Ring Closure

Flap with Buckled Straps

Flap with Tab Closure and Belted Detail

Flap Top with Tab/Slot Closure

Flap with Front Strap and Hidden Magnetic Closure

Flap with Turn Clasp and Lock

Fold-over Flap with Belted Strap

Fold-over Flap with Top Zipper and Magnetic Closure

BAG SIDES

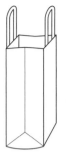

Gusset

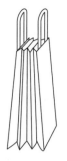

Accordion

Gusset Side with
Draw Strap

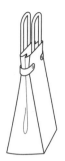

Button Tabs
on Sides

Side Panel
with Snap

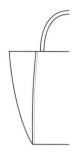

Winged Side

Zippered
Expandable Body

BAG CORNERS

Leather Corner

Shaped Leather Corner

Leather Corner with
Decorative Stitching

Metal Corner

Tassel Corner

Studded Corner

Multiple Stud Decorative
Corner

Buckle Corner

Reinforced Corner with
Screw Head

Zippered Corner

Eyelet Corner

Folded Corner

BAG BOTTOMS

Square Studded Bottom

Round Studded Bottom

5-Studded Bottom

6-Studded Bottom

Multiple Studded Bottom

Studded Bottom with
Corner Stitching

Studded Bottom with
Vertical Seam

Studded Bottom with
Horizontal Seam

Studded Bottom with
Reinforcement Tab

Envelope Bottom

Bottom with Corner
Guards

Extra Leather Bottom for
Reinforcement

BAG POCKETS

Flap Pocket

Flap Pocket with Snap Button

Saddle Pocket

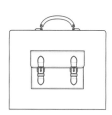

Double Strap Saddle Pocket

Loop and Button Pocket

Flap Pocket with Insert Loop

Kiss Lock Pocket

Shirred Patch Pocket

Zipper Gusset Pocket

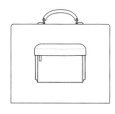

Zipper Gusset Pocket with
Hooded Cover

Zipper Pocket with
Leather End Tab

Zipper Pocket with Tassel

BAG INTERIOR DESIGN

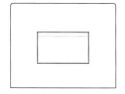

Open Pocket

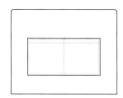

Divided Open Pocket

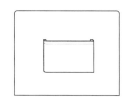

Expandable Gusset Open Pocket

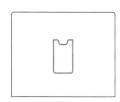

Credit Card Pocket

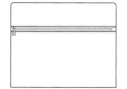

Full-sized Zipper Pocket

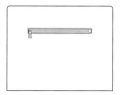

Half-sized Zipper Pocket

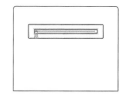

Zipper Pocket with Leather Trim

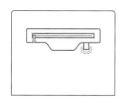

Zipper Pocket with Shaped
Leather Trim and Key Holder

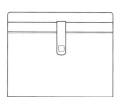

Laptop / Tablet Protective Pocket

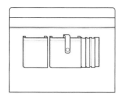

Laptop / Tablet Protective
Pocket with Phone, Charger
and Pen Holder

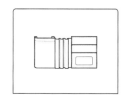

Phone Pocket with
Pen and Card Holder

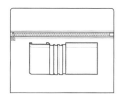

Full-sized Zipper Pocket with
Phone, Pen and Gadget Holder

BAG EMBELLISHMENTS & ACCESSORIES

PIN BUCKLES & SLIDERS

Buckle Set

Half Roller Buckle

Double Tongue Roller Buckle

Full Skate Buckle

Full Buckle

Half Buckle

Semi-circle Buckle

Circle Buckle

Oval Buckle

Western Buckle

Hexagon Buckle

Octagon Buckle

Belt Clasp

Full Slider

PLASTIC BUCKLES & SLIDERS

Side Release Buckle

Center Release Buckle

Tri-Glide

Strap Adjuster

Plastic D-Ring

Plastic Rectangle Ring

Reducing Loop

HOOKS & RINGS

Snap Hook

Bolt Snap Hook

Swivel Lobster Clasp

Heavy D-Ring

Light D-Ring

Unwelded D-Ring

Welded D-Ring

MAGNETIC SNAP BUTTONS

Prong Magnetic Snap

Sew-in Magnetic Snap

Concealed Magnetic Snap

Leather Based Sew-on Magnetic Snap

GROMMETS

Circle Shaped

Oval Shaped

Square Shaped

Floral Shaped

BAG / PURSE FRAMES

Glue-in Frame

Sew-in Frame

Internal Wire Bag Frame

Screw-in Frame

CORD EMBELLISHMENTS

Cord End

Cord Lock / Stopper

Double Cord Lock / Stopper

METAL CORNERS

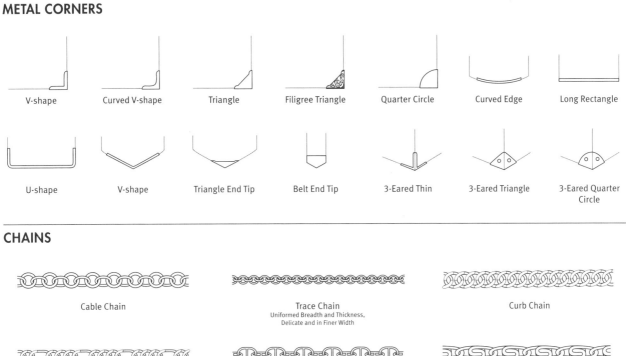

V-shape · Curved V-shape · Triangle · Filigree Triangle · Quarter Circle · Curved Edge · Long Rectangle

U-shape · V-shape · Triangle End Tip · Belt End Tip · 3-Eared Thin · 3-Eared Triangle · 3-Eared Quarter Circle

CHAINS

Cable Chain

Trace Chain
Uniformed Breadth and Thickness,
Delicate and in Finer Width

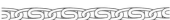

Curb Chain

Figaro Chain

Anchor Chain

Scroll Chain

Double Cable Chain

Foxtail Chain

Garibaldi Chain

Byzantine Chain

Double-link Cable Chain

Belcher Chain

Woven Leather Chain

Bar Chain

Venetian/Box Chain

Cocoon Chain

Snake Chain

Spiga Chain

Herringbone Chain

French Rope Chain

Cobra Chain

SEQUINS & BEADS

Cup Sequin · Flat Sequin · Large Paillette · Star Sequin · Heart Sequin · Leaf Sequin · Faceted Oval Bead · Faceted Round Bead

Seed Beads · Bugle Beads · Metal Bead · Wooden Ball · Navette Gemstone · Rectangular Gemstone · Pear Faceted Gemstone with Mount · Baguette Faceted Gemstone with Mount

ZIPPERS

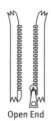
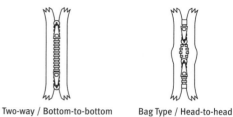

| Closed End | Open End | Invisible | Two-way / Bottom-to-bottom | Bag Type / Head-to-head |

ZIPPER TEETH

Molded Plastic Teeth

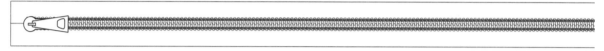

Nylon Coil Teeth

Metal Teeth

Waterproof

ZIPPER PULLS

| Non-lock Slider | Auto-lock Slider | Pin Lock Slider | Double Pull | Key Lock Slider | Cord Pull | Paracord Pull |

| Chain Pull | Tape Pull | Silicone Pull Faceted | Leather Pull | Self-knot Leather Pull | Braided Leather Pull | Tassel Pull |

BAG FEET / BASE STUDS

| Pyramid Rivet | Round Head | Cone-shaped Flat Top | Flat Top | Bifurcated | Square Rivet | Screw | Rockstud |

BAG LOCKS

Turn Lock

Double Turn Lock

Squeeze Lock

Combination Lock

Flip Lock

Push Lock / Press Lock

Lock and Key

Pin Lock

Pin Lock and Key

Toggle Clasp

Lock with Trigger Hook

Swing Lock

Kiss Lock

Safety Clasp

Celine Clasp Lock

Chanel CC Twist Lock

Chloe Turn Lock

Ferragamo Gancio Lock

Hermès Turn Lock

Louis Vuitton Squeeze Lock

Versace Lock and Key

METAL PLATES

Oval

Rectangle

Notched

Triangle

Stitched Leather Tag

Letter Logo

BAG CHARMS

Hanging Tassel

Logo Tag

Hanging Covered Key / Clochette Key Holder

Bag Charm

Mini Bag Fob

Pom Pom Bag Fob

Wrist Strap

Hook Strap Keychain

Luggage Tag

Handle Keeper

Retractable Cord Safety Rope

Carabiner

BAG ACCESSORIES

Shoulder Pad / Shoulder Guard

Luggage Handle Wrap

Purse Hook / Purse Hanger

Shoulder Strap Pocket

Waterproof Handbag Cover

Waterproof Backpack Cover

PART II

ANATOMY

ANATOMY

HANDBAG ANATOMY

Top Handle

Handle Holder / Handle Attachment Tab

Front Flap

Lock

Closure Strap

Gusset

Piping

Bag Tag / Fob

Base Studs / Feet / Protective Feet

EXPLODED VIEW OF A HANDBAG

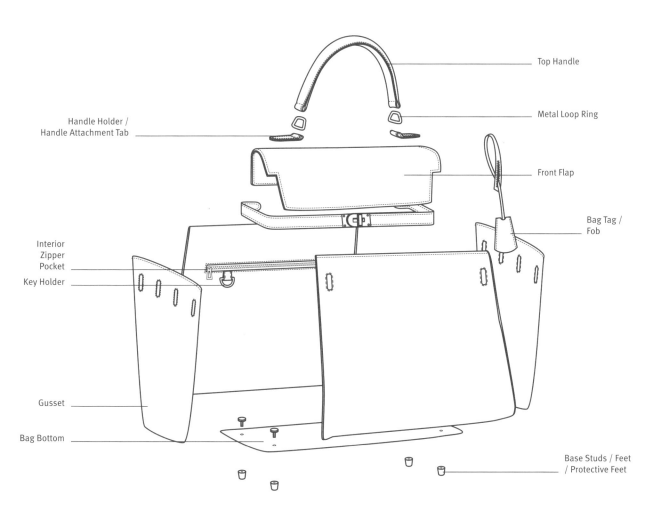

Top Handle

Handle Holder / Handle Attachment Tab

Metal Loop Ring

Front Flap

Interior Zipper Pocket

Key Holder

Bag Tag / Fob

Gusset

Bag Bottom

Base Studs / Feet / Protective Feet

CROSSBODY BAG ANATOMY

Metal Eyelet

Chain and Woven Leather Strap

Quilted Body

Front Flap

Press Lock

EXPLODED VIEW OF A CROSSBODY BAG

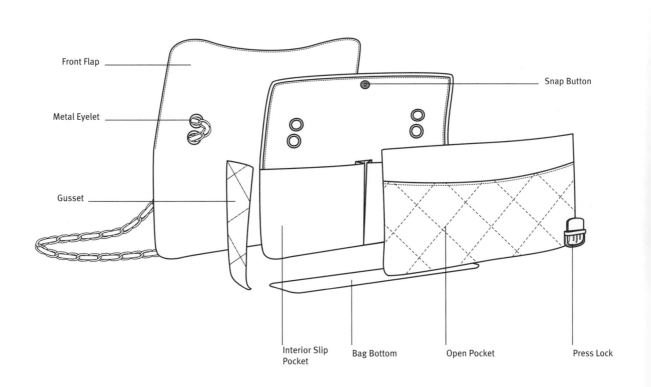

Front Flap

Metal Eyelet

Gusset

Snap Button

Interior Slip Pocket

Bag Bottom

Open Pocket

Press Lock

BACKPACK ANATOMY

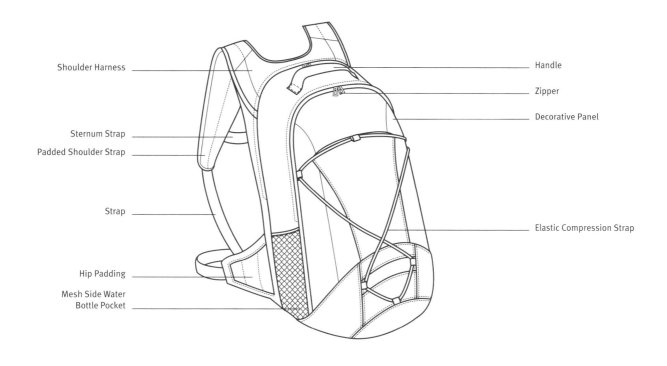

Shoulder Harness

Sternum Strap

Padded Shoulder Strap

Strap

Hip Padding

Mesh Side Water Bottle Pocket

Handle

Zipper

Decorative Panel

Elastic Compression Strap

EXPLODED VIEW OF A BACKPACK

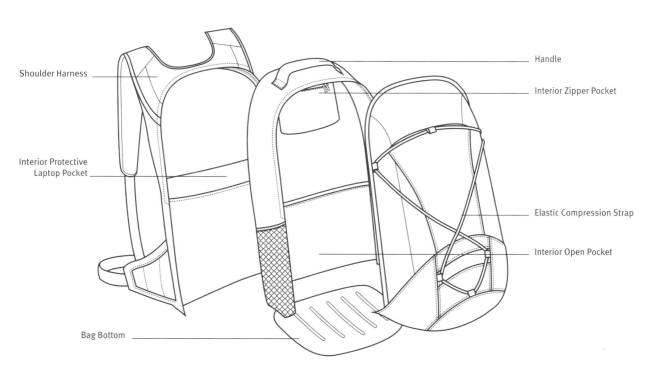

Shoulder Harness

Interior Protective Laptop Pocket

Bag Bottom

Handle

Interior Zipper Pocket

Elastic Compression Strap

Interior Open Pocket

CAMERA BAG ANATOMY

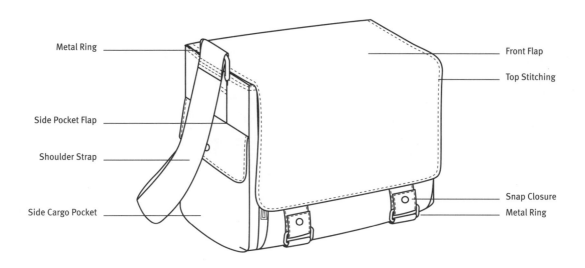

Metal Ring

Side Pocket Flap

Shoulder Strap

Side Cargo Pocket

Front Flap

Top Stitching

Snap Closure

Metal Ring

EXPLODED VIEW OF A CAMERA BAG

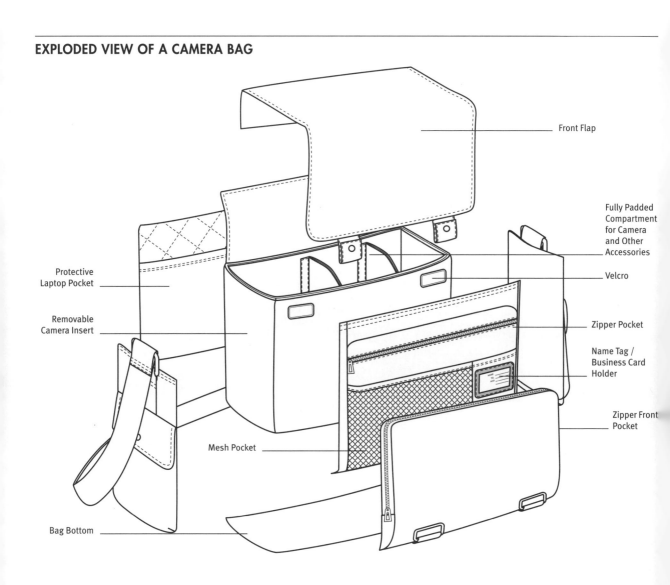

Front Flap

Fully Padded
Compartment
for Camera
and Other
Accessories

Protective
Laptop Pocket

Removable
Camera Insert

Velcro

Zipper Pocket

Name Tag /
Business Card
Holder

Zipper Front
Pocket

Mesh Pocket

Bag Bottom

LUGGAGE ANATOMY

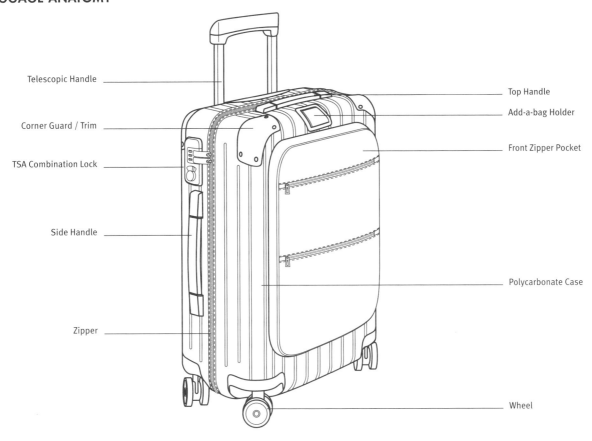

Telescopic Handle

Corner Guard / Trim

TSA Combination Lock

Side Handle

Zipper

Top Handle

Add-a-bag Holder

Front Zipper Pocket

Polycarbonate Case

Wheel

EXPLODED VIEW OF A LUGGAGE

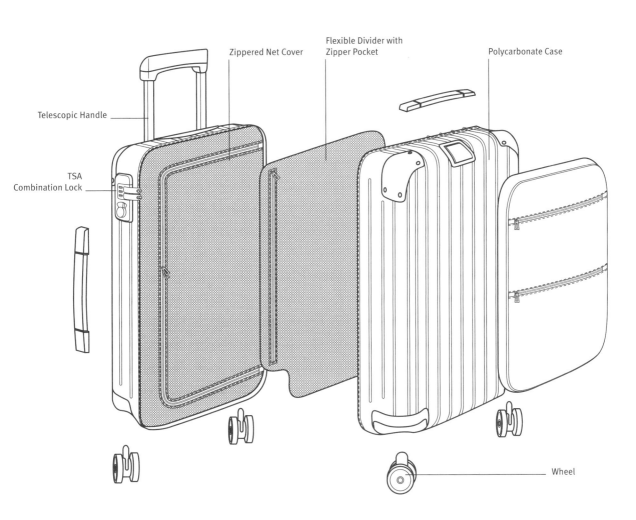

Telescopic Handle

TSA Combination Lock

Zippered Net Cover

Flexible Divider with Zipper Pocket

Polycarbonate Case

Wheel

ATTACHÉ CASE ANATOMY

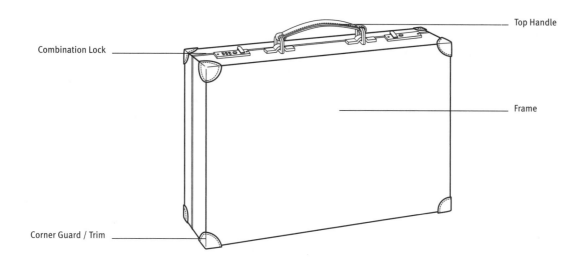

Combination Lock

Top Handle

Frame

Corner Guard / Trim

INTERIOR OF AN ATTACHÉ CASE

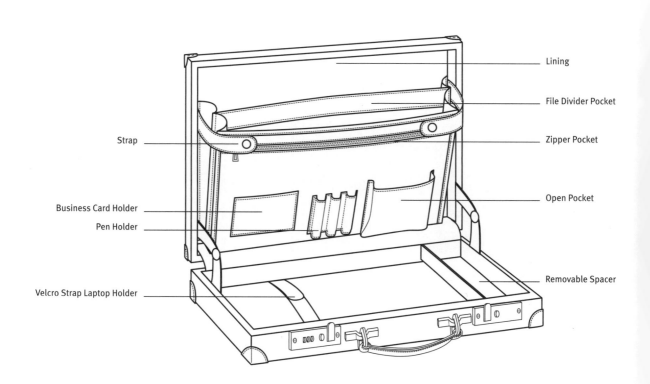

Strap

Business Card Holder

Pen Holder

Velcro Strap Laptop Holder

Lining

File Divider Pocket

Zipper Pocket

Open Pocket

Removable Spacer

BELT ANATOMY

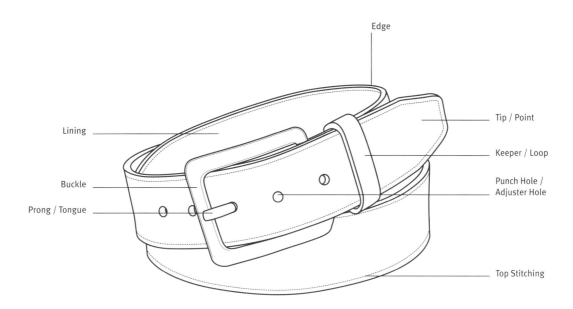

Edge

Lining

Buckle

Prong / Tongue

Tip / Point

Keeper / Loop

Punch Hole / Adjuster Hole

Top Stitching

WALLET ANATOMY

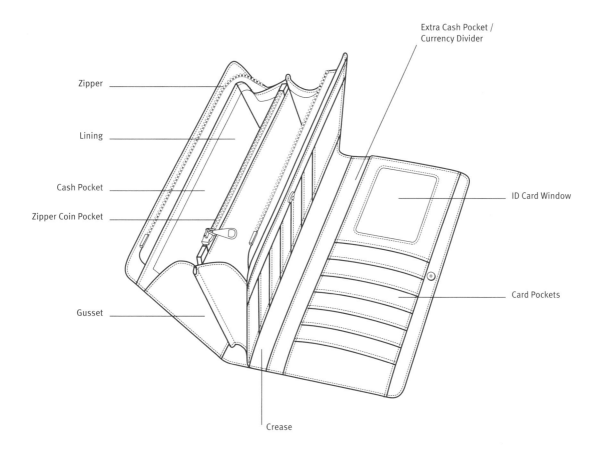

Extra Cash Pocket / Currency Divider

Zipper

Lining

Cash Pocket

Zipper Coin Pocket

ID Card Window

Gusset

Card Pockets

Crease

BAG MAKING

BAG MANUFACTURING PROCESS

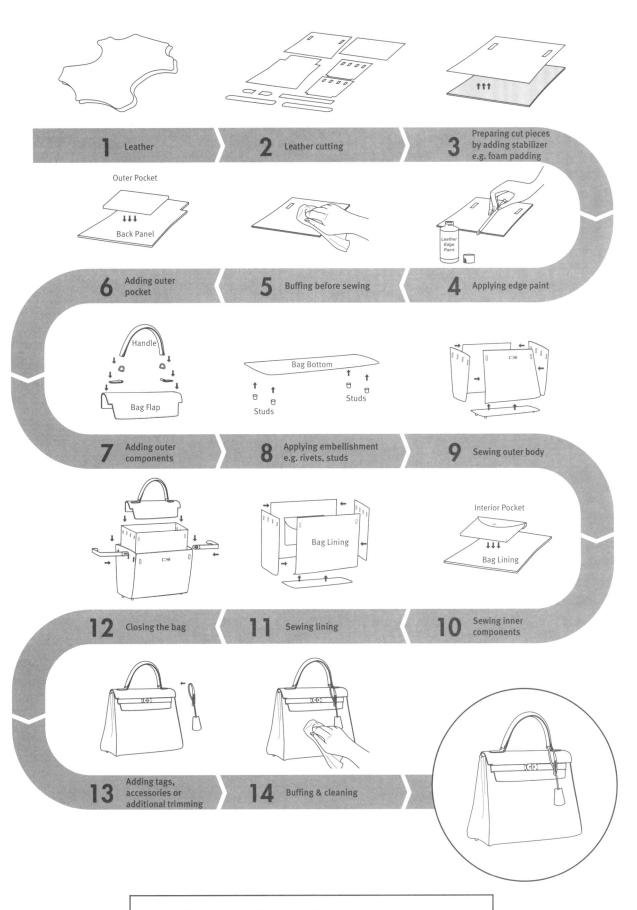

1 Leather

2 Leather cutting

3 Preparing cut pieces by adding stabilizer e.g. foam padding

Outer Pocket

Back Panel

Leather Edge Paint

6 Adding outer pocket

5 Buffing before sewing

4 Applying edge paint

Handle

Bag Flap

Bag Bottom

Studs

Studs

7 Adding outer components

8 Applying embellishment e.g. rivets, studs

9 Sewing outer body

Bag Lining

Interior Pocket

Bag Lining

12 Closing the bag

11 Sewing lining

10 Sewing inner components

13 Adding tags, accessories or additional trimming

14 Buffing & cleaning

Bag making videos on Fashionary Youtube Channel:
http://youtube.com/user/Fashionaryonline/playlists

BAG MAKING TOOLS

GENERAL BAG MAKING TOOLS

Dressmaking Scissors

Scissors specifically for cutting fabric.

Pinking Shears

Reduces the bulk of the seam and stops raw edges of fabric from fraying.

Duckbill / Appliqué Scissors

The flat, semi-circular shaped blade is designed to hold backing fabric. It can reduce the bulk of bag seams.

Rotary Point Cutter

With its point cutter and rounded blade, it can easily cut tight corners for bags.

Finger Presser

Used for pressing seams, pleats and tucks.

Loop Turner

A convenient tool for turning a fabric tube inside out to create a fabric strap.

Bodkin

It can be attached to a cord to quickly thread it through a fabric tube.

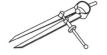

Compass

A measuring tool that can be opened to any required width and used to create a parallel line as a guide for cutting.

Thimble

Used for protecting the finger when hand-stitching.

Seam Ripper

Used for unpicking seams.

Pins

Used for keeping fabric together when sewing.

Hand-stitching Needle

Used for stitching in places where the sewing machine cannot reach.

Tailor's Chalk

Leaves marks before sewing.

Hera Marker

Creates subtle creases on fabric for easy stitching.

Pliers (For Hardware)

Opens or closes metal hardware e.g. for attaching chains onto a handbag

Grommet Plier

Designed to insert metal rings or eyelets.

Saddler's Punch

Used for punching holes of different sizes in fabric.

Steam Iron

Used for making perfect seams with its high heat and steam.

Ironing Board

Together with the steam iron, it is used for making perfect seams.

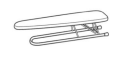

Sleeve Ironing Board

Used for seam pressing at the later stages of bag making.

Fabric Glue

An alternative way for sticking pieces together when sewing is not an option.

Basting Tape

Holds seams together when sewing.

Quilt Ruler

Create marks on fabric when making quilted fabric.

Measuring Tape

A flexible tape made from a non-stretch material.

Steel Ruler

A ruler strong enough to retain a perfect straight edge for cutting.

SEWING MACHINES & MACHINE FEET

Flat-bed Sewing Machine

A must-have tool for bag making. It is a machine used for stitching fabric and other materials together with thread.

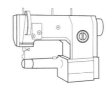

Cylinder Arm Sewing Machine

Once the bag takes on a shape, it gets harder to sew on a flat-bed machine. A cylinder arm machine would be a perfect alternative.

Even Feed Foot / Walking Foot

Used specifically for sewing multiple layers of fabric together.

Roller Foot

It has a roller attached and is used for sewing heavy seams or uneven surfaces.

Teflon / Leather Foot

Made of resin with a super smooth Teflon® coating on the sole of the foot, it is specifically used for sewing 'sticky' fabrics, e.g. leather, vinyl, PVC, suede, etc.

Piping Foot

The tunnel groove on the sole of the foot keeps the cords in position.

Zipper Foot

A foot used specifically for sewing zippers. It can be adjusted from left to right so the needle can stitch very close to the zipper.

1/4" Foot

Also known as a 'Patchwork foot', it has a built-in guide which keeps the fabric in exactly 1/4" position.

Free-motion Darning Foot

It gives maximum freedom for quilting or embroidering in any curve.

Clear Presser Foot

Being transparent, it offers maximum visibility and control especially when working with intricate designs.

LEATHER BAG MAKING TOOLS

Scalpel

A cutting knife with a very sharp blade, used for pattern cutting.

All Purpose Leather Knife

A knife used as a skiver. Round beveled, hand sharpened edges.

Rotary Cutter

Comprising a circular blade that rotates, it is a practical tool for achieving both straight and curved lines. It can easily cut through multiple layers of fabrics, which cannot be done precisely with scissors.

Leather Scissors

A pair of super sharp blades for cutting lighter weight leather.

Self-healing Cutting Mat

A self-healing synthetic cutting surface used for pattern cutting.

Brush

Used for brushing rubber adhesive on leather.

Rolling Spreader

For applying uniform pressure to the surface of adhesive.

Adhesive

A rubber solution that is used for attaching leather / fabric.

Leather Edge Paint

Gives a pleasing finish to the edges of leather.

Common Edge Tool

Bevels and rounds off edges of straps and all soft leather.

Multi-hole Punch

A punch for punching holes of different sizes on leather.

Masking Tape

An adhesive tape with a slight stretch.

Awl

A pointed tool used for piercing patterns or materials to create location points as a guide for cutting or stitching.

Glovers' Needle

Used for piercing and passing through tough materials such as leather, suede and vinyl without tearing.

Hammer

A small hammer used for setting rivets and eyelets.

BAG PATTERNS

ENVELOPE CLUTCH PATTERN

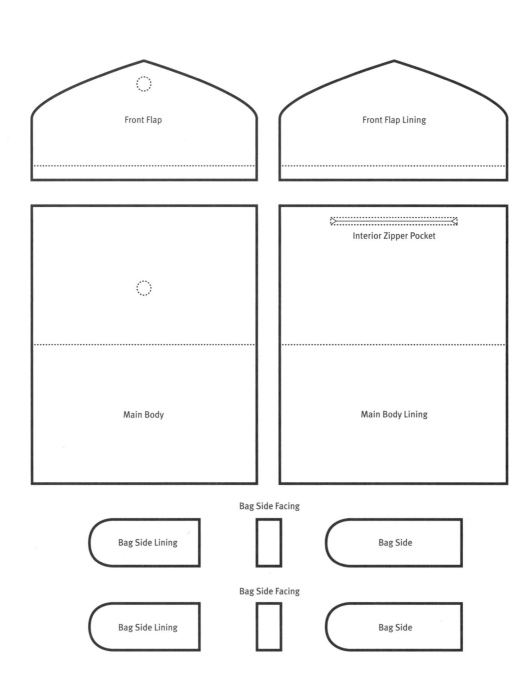

Front Flap

Front Flap Lining

Interior Zipper Pocket

Main Body

Main Body Lining

Bag Side Facing

Bag Side Lining

Bag Side

Bag Side Facing

Bag Side Lining

Bag Side

HANDBAG PATTERN

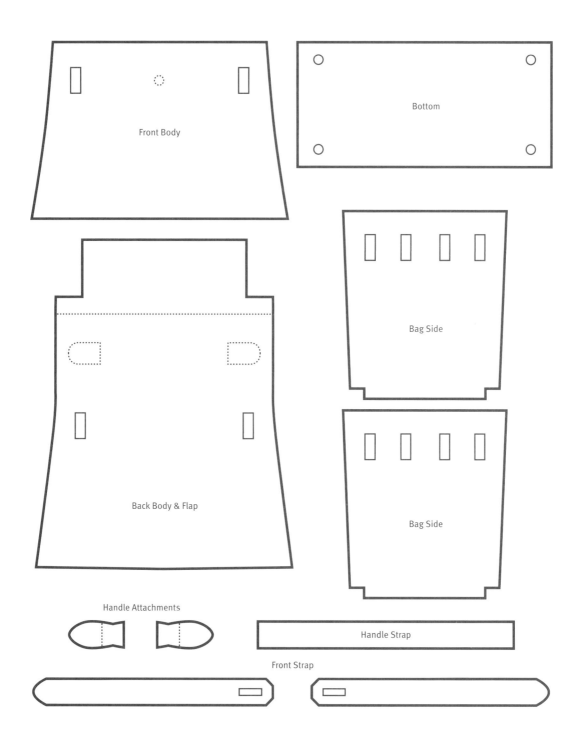

Front Body

Bottom

Back Body & Flap

Bag Side

Bag Side

Handle Attachments

Handle Strap

Front Strap

Main Body

Main Body Facing

Main Body Lining

Bottom

Bottom Lining

Strap

BOSTON BAG PATTERN

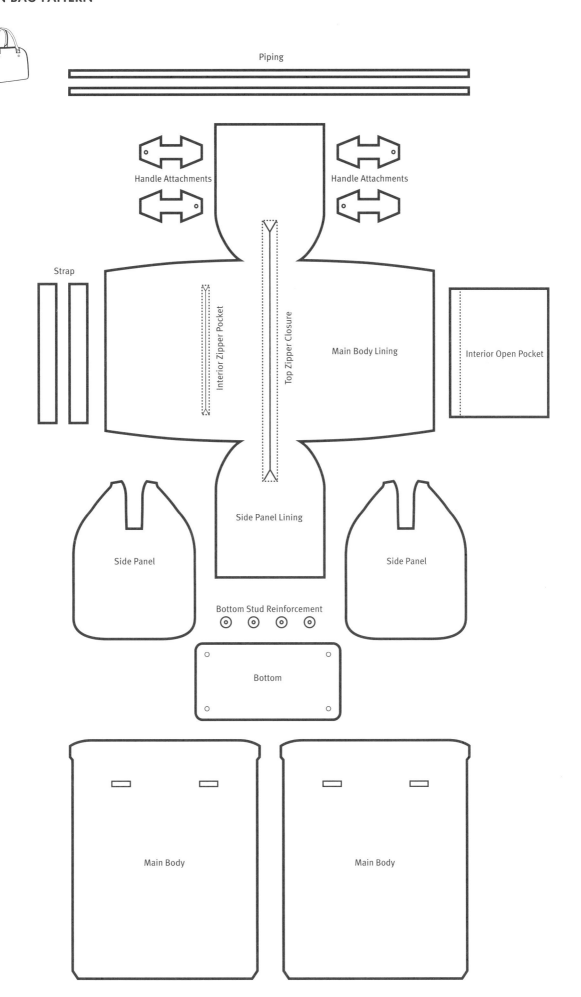

Piping

Handle Attachments

Handle Attachments

Strap

Interior Zipper Pocket

Top Zipper Closure

Main Body Lining

Interior Open Pocket

Side Panel Lining

Side Panel

Side Panel

Bottom Stud Reinforcement

Bottom

Main Body

Main Body

BRIEFCASE PATTERN

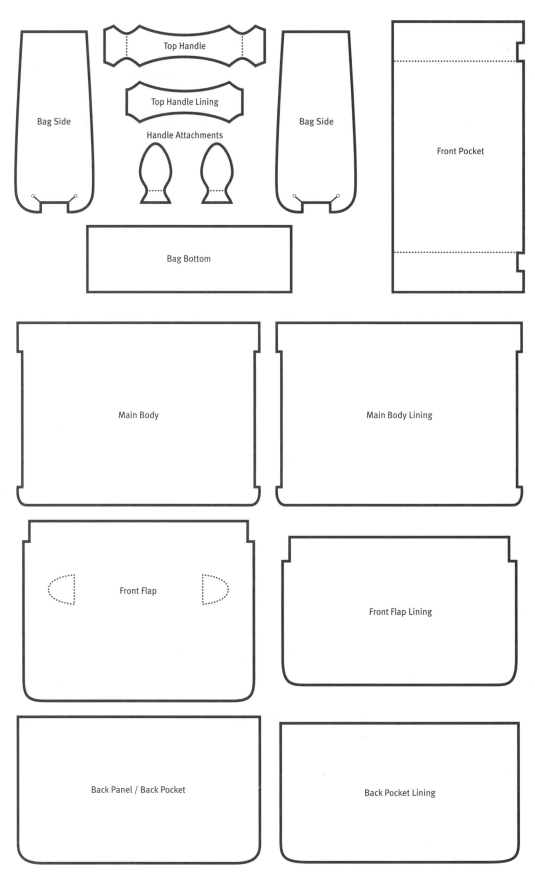

Top Handle

Top Handle Lining

Handle Attachments

Bag Side

Bag Side

Front Pocket

Bag Bottom

Main Body

Main Body Lining

Front Flap

Front Flap Lining

Back Panel / Back Pocket

Back Pocket Lining

BACKPACK PATTERN

Front Pocket Flap

Front Pocket

Front Pocket Lining

Front Pocket Gusset

Main Body Front

Handle Attachments

Strap Attachment on Bag Body

Back Strap Attachment Band

Main Body Back

Gusset Side / Bottom Panel

Gusset Side / Bottom Panel

Gusset Front Panel

Gusset Front Flap

Shoulder Strap

Shoulder Strap

PART IV

BAG LEATHERS & FABRICS

- LEATHER OVERVIEW
- COMMON LEATHER TYPES
- OTHER COMMON FABRICS FOR BAGS
- STABILIZER / INTERFACING FOR BAGS

LEATHER OVERVIEW

SUBDIVISIONS OF LEATHER

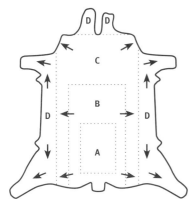

A - Butt ···································· Best Value, 13% of the hide
B - Bend ·································· Good Value, 30% of the hide
C - Shoulder ···························· Fair Value, 32% of the hide
D - Head, Belly ························· Poor Value, 25% of the hide
⟶ ·· Grain line

COMMON TANNING METHODS

Vegetable-tanned leather
Vegetable-tanned leather is tanned using tannins and other ingredients found in different vegetable matter, such as tree bark prepared in bark mills, wood, leaves, fruits and roots and other similar sources.

Chrome-tanned leather
Also known as wet blue, chrome tanning is the most common tanning method due to its cost and time needed. It is more supple and pliable than vegetable-tanned leather and does not discolor or lose shape as drastically in water as vegetable-tanned leather. More esoteric colors can be dyed.

Aldehyde-tanned leather
Also known as wet white, aldehyde tanning uses glutaraldehyde or oxazolidine compounds. The leather is often seen in automobiles and shoes for infants.

Rawhide
Rawhide is made by soaking thin skin into lime and then stretching it while it is dry. It is stiffer and more brittle than other forms of leather. It can be cut into cord and made into shoelaces.

CLASSIFICATION OF LEATHER

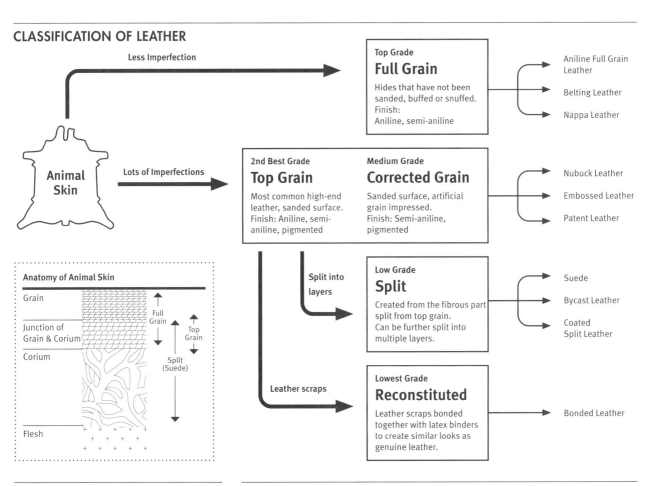

GRADING SYSTEM

A Grade	– No imperfection, marks or scars
B Grade	– 5-10% imperfection
C Grade	– 10-20% imperfection
D Grade	– 20-30% imperfection
E Grade	– 30-40% imperfection
F Grade	– Factory rejected

THICKNESS SYSTEM CONVERSION

Ounces	Thickness	Ounces	Thickness	Ounces	Thickness
1	0.4 mm	6	2.4 mm	11	4.4 mm
2	0.8 mm	7	2.8 mm	12	4.8 mm
3	1.2 mm	8	3.2 mm	13	5.2 mm
4	1.6 mm	9	3.6 mm	14	5.6 mm
5	2.0 mm	10	4.0 mm	15	6.0 mm

COMMON LEATHER TYPES

CATTLE

Most leather is made of cattle skin. Structure varies across the whole hide, strong.

Usage: A very common bag shell material

CALF

Slightly rubbery, fine grain, little variation across the skin.

Usage: Higher quality handbags

BUFFALO

Strong, tough, rubbery feel, pebbly appearance, thick.

Usage: Bag shell material, gloves

GOAT

Strong, thin, fine grain, regular pattern, papery feel.

Usage: Bag shell material, Balenciaga's The City

SHEEP

Good heat insulation. Thin, soft, loose fibrous structure. Loose grain surface and light substance with soft feel, very porous. Low durability.

Usage: Bag shell material, lining

LAMBSKIN

The softest, thinnest, most supple type of skin. Buttery texture and finely grained. Elastic, very form-fitting, stretches well and tends to reshape after wearing.

Usage: Luxury bag shell material, Chanel 2.55

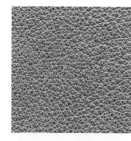

DEERSKIN

Tough, soft, supple, very stretchy. Washable and abrasion resistant.

Usage: Handbags, wallets

ELK

Similar to deerskin except very heavy and much thicker.

Usage: Bag shell material, wallets

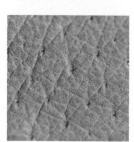

PIGSKIN

High breathability. Soft, thin, supple, durable, relatively tough with tight grain. Common hide for suede.

Usage: Quality bag shell material

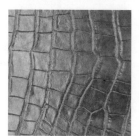

ALLIGATOR

Thick in the bend and thin in the belly and limbs. Scaly, supple (belly), tough, durable.

Usage: Luxury bag shell material, Hermès Kelly

SNAKE

Great variation according to the type of snake, distinctive pattern, lightweight, strong, papery feel.

Usage: Luxury bag shell material, decoration

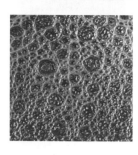

FROG / TOAD

Lightweight, thin, strong, great variation depending on the species.

Usage: Bag shell material, decoration

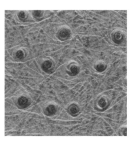

OSTRICH

One of the finest and most durable types of skins in the world. Unique bumpy texture. Flexible, pliable, durable and soft, very strong.

Usage: Bag shell material, favored by many major fashion houses such as Hermès, Prada, Gucci, and Louis Vuitton

KANGAROO

Very strong (10 times the tensile strength of cowhide and is 50% stronger than goatskin), thin, lightweight, uniform fiber structure.

Usage: High performance motorcycle leather

SALMON

Fine scales, pliable, strong and elegant looking. The most popular fish leather

Usage: Wallets, handbag

PERCH

Sourced from the Nile. Thick, large and soft round scales.

Usage: Wallets, purses

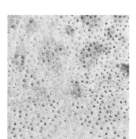

WOLFFISH

Smooth skin, scaleless. Easily recognizable thanks to its dark spots and 'stripes' which are due to the friction of marine rocks.

Usage: Belts, wallets

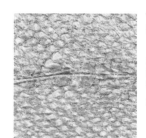

COD

Its skin has finer scales than salmon, but its texture is more varied, sometimes smooth and sometimes rough.

Usage: Wallets, purses

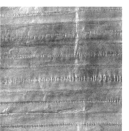

EEL

Very smooth in touch with an elegant horizontal pinstripe-like pattern. Lightweight, supple, incredibly strong. Sewn together to create a leather panel.

Usage: Handbags and wallets with distinctive stripe pattern

TILAPIA

Compared with salmon skin, the pattern of tilapia leather is more beautiful, but the skins are smaller in size.

Usage: Wallets, purses

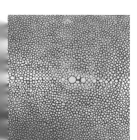

STINGRAY

Distinctive pattern. Highly durable (25 times more durable than cowhide leather) and has a unique supple texture.

Usage: Bag shell material, wallets and belts

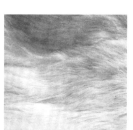

RABBIT

Small in size, thin and fragile.

Usage: Handbag shell material, decoration

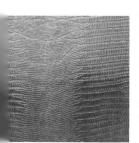

LIZARD

Strong, lightweight, papery feel and thin.

Usage: Luxury bag shell material, decoration

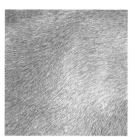

HORSE

Tough, thin, non-uniform quality, stretches well. Commonly used for making shoes.

Usage: Bag shell material

OTHER COMMON FABRICS FOR BAGS

COTTON CANVAS

An inexpensive heavyweight, rough woven cotton material.

Usage: Any type of bags, casual totes

DENIM

Originally used in workwear or jeans, denim has a stone-washed effect that could be applied to the bag design.

Usage: Casual bags, backpacks

STRAW

One of the oldest materials for bag making, straw can be woven into bags.

Usage: Beach bags

PATENT LEATHER

Unlike standard leather, patent leather has a shiny mirror-like finish and comes in a wider variety of colors.

Usage: Medium priced bags or other small leather goods

FAUX LEATHER

Most commonly made of plastic, it is not as durable as real leather, but it is water-resistant. It has a broader color range than real leather since it is a man-made leather.

Usage: Low to medium priced bags or other small leather goods

SUEDE

It is made from the underside of animal skin, and is not as durable as standard leather. Unlike leather, suede tends to absorb liquids readily, and therefore stains easily.

Usage: Medium priced bags

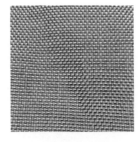

CORDURA

An 'air treated' rough nylon fabric originally designed by DuPoint, famous for it water repellency, durability and abrasion resistance.

Usage: Backpacks, daypacks, functional bags

NYLON PACKCLOTH

A smooth and shiny nylon material that is slick to the touch.

Usage: Backpacks, functional bags

RIPSTOP NYLON

With its signature 'grid' pattern, it is a lightweight nylon fabric famous for its resistance to tearing.

Usage: Backpacks, functional bags

BALLISTIC NYLON

A thick and durable synthetic nylon fabric which is very easy to clean.

Usage: Softside luggage, backpacks, functional bags

PVC FABRIC

A durable and colorful fabric that can be used to add color, durability and waterproof properties.

Usage: Wash bags, waterproof bag, decoration

MESH FABRIC

Mostly made of nylon or polyester, it is lightweight, thin, strong, and is available in a wide variety of styles.

Usage: Functional bags, decoration

STABILIZER / INTERFACING FOR BAGS

COTTON / POLYESTER BATTING

Made with glue or bonding adhesive, it is used as a layer of insulation between fabrics, and can be used in quilt making. It adds warmth and a heavy touch to the fabric.

Usage: Luxury handbags, quilted bags

SPUNLACE FABRIC

Spunlacing uses high-speed jets of water so the fibers get knotted to one another and form the fabric shape. It is always used as the backing of PVC leather for keeping the shape of the fabric

Usage: Low to medium priced bags, PVC leather

WOVEN / NONWOVEN INTERFACING

Fusible or sew-in interfacing are often used in bag making for adding stiffness and keeping the bag in shape.

Usage: Any type of bags

REGENERATED LEATHER FIBERBOARD

Also known as 'bonded leather', it is made of the wasted part of the leather. Has high elasticity, strength and water resistance.

Usage: Luxury handbags

EVA FOAM PADDING

Ethylene-vinyl acetate (EVA), also known as 'expanded rubber' or 'foam rubber', is popular for its shock absorption. It is often used as the middle layer of backpack straps.

Usage: Backpack straps

PVC COATING

Instead of adding an extra layer of stabilizer, PVC coating on the surface of the fabric could make it waterproof and resistant to dirt, mildew, oil and UV rays, and can also increase the stability and strength of the bag.

Usage: Backpacks, functional bags, casual totes

PART V

BAG CARE
& BUYING

BAG CARE TOOLS

LEATHER BAG CARE TOOLS

Leather Cleaner

Effectively removes dust and dirt from leather.

Leather Conditioner

Lubricates and protects all top-coated/protected leather. Makes leather look and feel like new.

Saddle Soap

Used for cleaning, conditioning and softening leather, particularly that of saddles and other horse tack.

pH Balanced Leather Cleaner

Matches the pH of your leather to better preserve the leather's strength, durability and appearance.

Cream Polish

Protects and nourishes leather to produce a long-lasting glossy shine similar to that of satin.

Suede Cleaner

Effectively removes dust and dirt from all types of suede and nubuck leathers.

Suede Protector

Provides maximum protection against water and stains, for suede and nubuck leather.

Exotic Leather Cleaner

Used for cleaning exotic leathers such as alligator, snake, lizard, ostrich, eel, etc.

Patent Leather Cleaner

Used for cleaning patent leather.

All Purpose Leather Cleaner & Conditioner

Cleans and preserves grained, gloved, patent, and smooth leathers.

CARE TOOLS FOR OTHER FABRICS

Mild Liquid Soap

Can be applied to any type of bags for cleaning light dirt and mold.

Mild Bar Soap

Can be applied to any type of bags with for cleaning light dirt and mold.

LUGGAGE CARE TOOLS

Polish & Repair Paste

For polishing plastic luggage shells, and to clean spots, scratches and abrasions.

Brake Cleaner

For polishing metallic luggage shells, especially aluminum.

Multi-purpose Oil

Used when the wheel of the luggage is not working smoothly.

BRUSHES & CLEANING CLOTHS

Shine Cloth

The cloth brings up a brilliant shine after polishing and spit shining.

Horsehair Shine Brush

Used for buffing leather products to a high shine.

Horse Hair Circular Dauber Brush

The brush can spread shoe polish evenly and thoroughly.

Cleaning Sponge

For general cleaning purposes.

Microfiber Cloth

When there is no water or soap, a microfiber cloth works great on removing oil and dirt.

OTHER BAG CARE PRODUCTS

Stain & Water Repellent Spray

Provides an invisible protective coating that repels water and stains to keep the bag clean and dry.

Dustbag

Protects the bag from dust and prevents color transfer during storage.

Storage Box

Used for bag storage to prevent damage to its shape.

Bubble Wrap

Used for filling up the bag to maintain its shape during storage.

Silica Gel

Used to control humidity and keep mold away.

BAG CARE & MAINTENANCE

HOW TO USE A SHINE CLOTH

Remove dirt on the leather bag

Use 3 fingers to hold the shine cloth and rub on the bag.

Apply leather cleaner on the bag

Fold the shine cloth into quarters. Use 3 fingers to hold the shine cloth and rub on the bag for polishing.

Apply leather conditioner

Use 2 fingers to hold the shine cloth and rub on the bag gently.

Bringing up shine after polishing

Fold the shine cloth into its thickest. Hold the cloth in your fist and rub on the bag gently.

LEATHER BAG CARE

Tools required:

Horsehair Shine Brush · · · · ·
Shine Cloth · · · · · · · · · · · · · ·
Leather Cleaner · · · · · · · · · · ·
Leather Conditioner · · · · · · · ·

  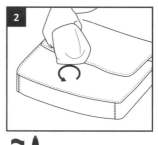 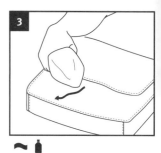

Remove any dirt/mud/salt with a brush or damp rag. Wait until dry.

Apply leather cleaner in small circles, in small amounts.

Apply leather conditioner and rub it gently.

GENERAL BAG CARE ON A DAILY BASIS

Tools required:

Horsehair Shine Brush · · · · ·

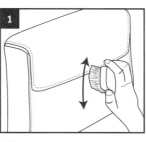 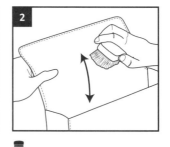

Remove any dirt/mud/salt on the surface of the bag with a brush or damp rag.

Open the bag to clean the inside with the brush or damp rag. Do it everyday after use.

NYLON BAG CARE

Tools required:

Liquid Soap · · · · · · · · · · · · · ·
Microfiber Cloth · · · · · · · · · · ·
Warm Water · · · · · · · · · · · · · ·

Mix 2 cups of warm water (500ml) with a few drops of liquid soap.

Dip a microfiber cloth in the soapy water and wring out the excess moisture.

Clean any dirt/mud/salt on the surface of the bag with the damp microfiber cloth.

COTTON CANVAS BAG CARE

Tools required:

Liquid Soap ⋯⋯⋯⋯⋯
Cold Water ⋯⋯⋯⋯⋯

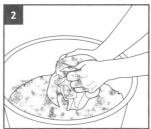

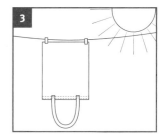

Mix cold water with a few drops of liquid soap. Cold water will prevent the bag from shrinking.

Wash the cotton canvas bag by hand. Make sure to rinse the soap out before hanging.

Reshape the canvas tote then hang to dry. Do not put a canvas tote bag in a dryer

ALUMINUM LUGGAGE CARE

Tools required:

Liquid Soap ⋯⋯⋯⋯⋯
Cold Water ⋯⋯⋯⋯⋯
Microfiber Cloth ⋯⋯⋯⋯
Brake Cleaner ⋯⋯⋯⋯

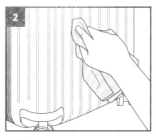

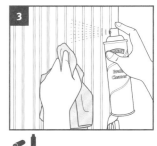

Mix cold water with a few drops of liquid soap. Dip a microfiber cloth in the soapy water and wring out the excess moisture.

Remove any dirt/mud/salt with the damp cloth. Wait until dry.

Use brake cleaner to clean the dirt inside the scratches.

REMOVING MOLD ON A BAG

Tools required:

Cold Water ⋯⋯⋯⋯⋯
1:1 Vinegar & Water ⋯⋯⋯
Microfiber Cloth ⋯⋯⋯⋯

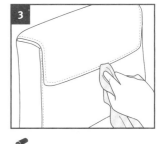

Wet the microfiber cloth and rub the moldy area on the bag until it is clean.

Mix equal parts of vinegar and water.

Dampen a cloth with the mixture and use it to wipe the surface.

REMOVING A STICKER ON LUGGAGE

Tools required:

Hair Dryer ⋯⋯⋯⋯⋯

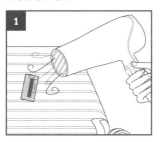

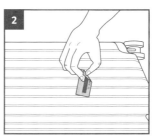

Blow hot air on the sticker for around 45 seconds.

Peel off the sticker from one corner. If it is still lodged on, heat it for another 30-45 seconds and try again.

PART VI

MISCELLANEOUS

COMMON LOGO PLACEMENT POSITIONS

CLUTCH & HANDHELD BAGS

CROSSBODY & SHOULDER BAGS

BACKPACKS & WAIST BAGS

BOOKS & BOOKMARKS

BOOKS

Bag Making

- 25 More Bags to Knit: Beautiful Bags in Stylish Colors
- A Bag for All Reasons: 12 all-new bags and purses to sew for every occasion
- A Guide to Making Leather Handbags
- Amy Butler's Style Stitches: 12 Easy Ways to 26 Wonderful Bags
- Bag Style: 20 Inspirational Handbags, Totes, and Carry-alls to Knit and Crochet
- Bags for Fashionistas: Designing, Sewing, Selling
- Bags in Bloom: Create 20 Unique Flower Purses with Simple Embroidery Stitches and Easy-to-Sew Patterns
- Bags, The Modern Classics: Clutches, Hobos, Satchels & More
- Big-City Bags: Sew Handbags with Style, Sass, and Sophisticatio
- Carry Me
- Chic Bags: 22 Handbags, Purses, Totes, and Accessories to Make
- Complete Leatherwork: Easy Techniques and Over 20 Great Projects
- Creating Romantic Purses: Patterns & Instructions for Unique Handbags
- Duct Tape Bags
- Easy-to-Sew Handbags: wristlets, clutches & beautiful bags
- Fat Quarter Bags
- Felted Bags, Boots & Other Things: 56 Projects
- Felted Bags: 30 Original Bag Designs to Knit and Felt
- Handbag Workshop: Design and Sew the Perfect Bag
- Handmade Bags In Natural Fabrics: Over 25 Easy-To-Make Purses, Totes and More
- Handmade Bags: How to Design, Create and Embellish Beautiful Bags
- Handmade Chic: Fashionable Projects That Look High-End, Not Homespun
- Hip Handbags: Creating & Embellishing 40 Great-Looking Bags
- Lion Brand Yarn: Just Bags: 30 Patterns to Knit and Crochet

- Making Leather Handbags and Other Stylish Accessories
- Making Vinyl, Plastic, and Rubber Handbags
- On the Go Bags - 15 Handmade Purses, Totes & Organizers
- Patchwork Bags (Love to Sew)
- Purses, Bags & More
- Refashioned Bags: Upcycle Anything into High-Style Handbags
- Sew Serendipity Bags: Fresh and Pretty Projects to Sew and Love
- Sew What! Bags: 18 Pattern-Free Projects You Can Customize to Fit Your Needs
- Sewing Leather Accessories
- Sewing Pretty Little Things: How to Make Small Bags and Clutches from Fabric Remnants
- Simply Stylish Bags: 18 Stunning Designs for All Occasions
- Terrific Totes & Carryalls: 40 Bags to Sew for Shopping, Working, Hiking, Biking, and More
- The Bag Making Bible
- The Handbag: An Illustrated History
- The Hip Handbag Book: 25 Easy-to-Make Totes, Purses, and Bags
- The Perfect Handmade Bag: Recycle and Reuse to Make 35 Beautiful Totes, Purses, and More
- Totes Amaze: 25 Bags to Make for Every Occasion

Brand Background

- Bottega Veneta
- Braccialini: Bags in Wonderland
- Fendi Baguette
- Louis Vuitton City Bags: A Natural History

Production / Technical

- 1,000 Bags, Tags, and Labels
- Accessory Design
- Handmade Leather Bags & Accessories
- How to Sew Leather, Suede, Fur
- Leather Braiding
- Lunch Bags!
- Perfect Patchwork Bags
- Simple Bags Japanese Style

- The Better Bag Maker
- The Leatherworking Handbook
- Vintage Purses to Make, Sew & Embroidery

Reference

- A Century of Handbags: The Modern Handbag for Antique Lovers
- A Passion for Purses: 1600-2005
- Art of the Handbag: Crazy Beautiful Bags
- Bag and Shoe Design: Hester van Eeghen
- Bag: The Ultimate Fashion Accessory
- Bags
- Bags That Rock: Knitting on the Road with Kelley Deal
- Bags to Love: In Pop-Up
- Bags: A Selection from the Museum of Bags and Purses, Amsterdam
- Exotic Skin: Alligator and Crocodile Handbags
- Fifty Bags That Changed the World
- Fun Handbags
- Handbag Chic: 200 Years of Designer Fashion
- Handbag Designer 101
- Handbags
- Handbags: 900 Bags to Die For
- Handbags: A Peek Inside A Woman's Most Trusted Accessory
- Handbags: The Making of a Museum
- High Fashion Handbags: Classic Vintage Designs
- Judith Leiber: The Artful Handbag
- Luxe Fashion: A Tribute to the World's Most Enduring Labels
- Purse Masterpieces Identification and Value Guide
- The Belt
- The Handbag: To Have and to Hold
- Vintage Handbags
- Warman's Handbags Field Guide: Values & Identification

Theory

- Basics Fashion Design 09: Designing Accessories
- Encyclopedia of Fashion Accessories
- Encyclopedia of Rawhide and Leather Braiding
- Fashion Design Course: Accessories
- Start Your Own Fashion Accessories Business
- The Secret History of the Handbag

BOOKMARKS

Bag Blogs

bagaholicboy.com
bagbible.com
bagbliss.com
bags.stylosophy.it
bellabag.com/blog
blog.chriswdesigns.com
blog.queenbeeofbeverlyhills.com
carryology.com
celebritybagstyles.com
damselindior.com
deni-deni.com/blog
designerbagsanddirtydiapers.blogspot.com
notey.com/blogs/designer-bags
portero.com/blog
purseblog.com
pursepage.com
snobessentials.com
thebagblog.com

Leather Goods Blogs

asailorsleather.blogspot.com
fineleatherworking.com/blog
goldbarkleather.com/blog
horween.com/blog
mrlentz.com
peartreeleather.com/blog
pedsnro.blogspot.hk

Bag Information / History

bforbag.com
henriettashandbags.com
thepursemuseum.com
thesack.org
thisoldtrunk.com

Leather Information

basader.com/blog
leatherhouse.com
leatherlearn.com
leathersmithdesigns.com
neumannleathers.com

Bag Making

bagntell.wordpress.com
bags-to-sew.com/blog
bagsyoucanmake.blogspot.com
cloverandviolet.com
craftpassion.com
emmalinebags.blogspot.com
sewchristine.blogspot.com
sewsweetness.com
sweetbeebuzzings.blogspot.com
thesewingdirectory.co.uk/bag-making-techniques
u-handbag.typepad.com

TRADE FAIRS, MUSEUMS & COURSES

FASHION ACCESSORIES & LEATHER TRADE FAIRS

Canada	Toronto	Moda Accessories	Accessories	Jan/Aug	mode-accessories.com
China	Shanghai	All China Leather Exhibition	Leather	Sep	acle.aplf.com
	Shanghai	Chic / China Int'l Clothing and Accessories Fair	Apparel, Accessories	Mar/Oct	chiconline.com.cn
	Shanghai	Intertextile Shanghai	Apparel, Fabrics	Mar/Oct	intertextileapparel.com
	Shanghai	Shanghai International Bags Leather Handbags Exhibition	Accessories	May	en.cshbox.com
	Shenzhen	Shenzhen International Trade Fair for Apparel Fabrics and Accessories	Accessories, Fabrics	Jul	hk.messefrankfurt.com
Czech Republic	Brno	KABO	Leather, Accessories	Jan/Aug	bvv.cz/kabo
France	Paris	Accessoires De Mode	Accessories	Apr	foiredeparis.fr
	Paris	Première Classe	Accessories	Mar/Jul/Oct	premiere-classe.com
Germany	Düsseldorf	Tag it!	Accessories	Mar/Jul	tag-it-show.com
	Düsseldorf	The Gallery Düsseldorf	Apparel, Accessories	Mar/Jul	gallery-duesseldorf.de
Hong Kong	Hong Kong	APLF Leather & Material	Leather	Mar	leatherfair.aplf.com
	Hong Kong	Fashion Access	Accessories, Footwear	Apr/Oct	fashionaccess.aplf.com
	Hong Kong	The Global Sources Fashion show	Accessoires	Mar/Sep	globalsources.com
India	Mumbai	India Shoes and Accessories Forum	Accessories, Footwear	Mar	isaf.in
Iran	Tehran	Iran FashionExpo	Apparel, Accessories	Mar/Sep	iranfashionexpo.com
Italy	Milan	Mipap	Apparel, Accessories	Mar/Sep	mipap.it
	Milan	Mipel	Leather	Mar/Sep	mipel.com
	Milan	SUPER	Apparel, Accessories	Mar/Sep	pittimmagine.com/corporate/fairs/super.html
Japan	Tokyo	Fashion Goods & Accessories Expo	Accessories	Jul	fa-expo.jp/en
	Tokyo	Tokyo Bag Expo	Accessories	Apr/Nov	bag-expo.jp
Poland	Poznan	Next Season	Apparel, Accessories	Jan/Aug	next-season.mtp.pl
Romania	Bucharest	Modexpo	Apparel, Accessories	Mar/Oct	modexpo.ro
Russia	Moscow	CPM. Collection Premiere	Apparel, Accessories	Mar/Sep	cpm-moscow.com
	Moscow	Garderobe	Accessories	Apr/Oct	garderobe-expo.ru/en
Spain	Madrid	International Fashion Jewellery and Accessories Trade Fair	Accessories	Mar/Sep	ifema.es/bisutex_06
Sweden	Stockholm	Nordic Shoe & Bag Fair	Accessories	Aug	stockholmfashiondistrict.se
Turkey	Istanbul	Aymod	Accessories, Footwear	Apr/Nov	cnraymod.com
UK	Birmingham	Moda - Footwear	Apparel, Accessories	Feb/Aug	moda-uk.co.uk
	Birmingham	Spring Fair	Accessories, Gift	Feb/Aug	springfair.com
	London	Pure London	Apparel, Accessories	Feb/Aug	purelondon.com
US	New York	Accessorie Circuit	Accessories	Jan/Aug	enkshows.com/circuit
	New York	Accessories the Show NY	Accessories	Jan/Aug	accessoriestheshow.com
	New York / Las Vegas	Capsule	Apparel, Accessories	Jan/Feb	capsuleshow.com
Vietnam	Ho Chi Minh City	IFLE - Vietnam	Leather, Footwear	Jul	ifle-vietnam.com

BAG & ACCESSORIES MUSEUMS

France
Musée De La Mode Et Du Textile, Paris

Musée Galliera, Paris

Japan
World Bags and Luggage Museum, Tokyo

Korea
Simone Handbag Museum, Seoul

The Netherlands
The Museum of Bags and Purses, Amsterdam

UK
The British Museum, London

Victoria & Albert Museum, London

US
Costume Institute, New York

ESSE Purse Museum, Little Rock

FIDM Museum, California

The Metropolitan Museum of Art, New York

The Museum at FIT, New York

BAG & ACCESSORIES COURSES

Italy
Istituto Marangoni, Milan
- Fashion Design & Accessories

Polimoda, Florence
- Undergraduate in Footwear and Accessories Design

Japan
Bunka Fashion College, Tokyo
- Accessories Design Course in Fashion Accessories and Textiles Department

UK
De Montfort University, Lecester
- BA (Hons) in Fashion Textiles and Accessories

London College of Fashion, London
- BA (Hons) Cordwainers Fashion Bags and Accessories

Nottingham Trent University, Nottingham
- BA (Hons) Fashion Accessory Design

Ravensbourne, London
- BA (Hons) in Fashion Accessory Design and Prototyping

University of Northampton, Northampton
- BA (Hons) Fashion (Footwear and Accessories)

US
The Fashion Institute of Technology, NY
- Bachelor of Fine Arts (BFA) degree in Accessories Design

BAG SPEC SHEET

Date	6th, August	Product Name	Baguette Bag	Thread
Deadline	1st, October	Product Number	SS 1832 0001	Finish 1
Company	Fashionary Company	Last Model	Spring Line, #P412	Finish 2
Season	Spring Summer			Nylon 60 Brown

A Front or ¾ View

6.5cm

2

1

B Back View

14cm
14.5cm
24cm

C Bottom View

6cm
1

D Side View

2cm

E Inside Front

10cm

F Inside Back

17cm

Description

	Material	Description	
Front Body	Brown Calf Leather	Colour Code: BR002	
Back Body	Brown Calf Leather	Colour Code: BR002	
Gusset	Brown Calf Leather	Colour Code: BR002	
Bottom			
Top Handle	Brown Calf Leather	Colour Code: BR002	
Lining	Khaki Cotton Fabric	Colour Code: KA003	
Flap Lining	Brown Cotton Lamb	Colour Code: BR002	
Front Buckle	Silver Full Buckle	Buckle Code: EBS305	
Side Buckle	Silver Half Buckle	Buckle Code: EBS502	
Hidden Snap	Silver Hidden Snap	Snap Code: ESS102	

Notes

A	B	C	D	E	F
1. 3mm top stitching 2. Hidden magnetic snap		1. 3mm top stitching		10cm width mobile phone inside pocket	Leather trimmed inside zipper place in the middle

RANGE PLAN

Company :	Fashionary Company			Season :	Spring Summer			
Product		Material	Lining	Closure	Buckle	Colourway	Price
Product Number: SS 1832 0001		Calf Leather	100% Cotton Lining Fabric	Hidden Magnetic Snap Metal Teeth Zipper (Nickel) Zipper Pull (Nickel) X 1pc	Full Slider (Nickel) X 1 pair Half Buckle (Nickel) X 2 pcs	Colourway #1 Upper: Brown - BR003 Lining: Khaki - KA003 Colourway #2 Upper: Black - BK001 Lining: Red - RE002	US$239
Product Number: SS 1832 0002		Calf Leather	100% Cotton Lining Fabric	Hidden Magnetic Snap		Colourway #1 Upper: Red - RE005 Lining: Cream- CR002 Colourway #2 Upper: White - WH001 Lining: White - WH001	US$329
Product Number: SS 1832 0003		Calf Leather	100% Cotton Lining Fabric	Metal Teeth Zipper Zipper Pull (Nickel) X 2pcs	Plastic D-ring X 1 pair Half Buckle (Nickel) X 1 pc	Colourway #1 Upper: Blue - BL004 Lining: Blue - BL004 Colourway #2 Upper: Black - BK001 Lining: Red - RE002	US$289

Download the range plan - http://fashionary.org/downloads

BAG GLOSSARY

Accordion
/ A type of internal construction found in handbags and briefcases, where the compartment folds open like accordion bellows.

Aniline Leather
/ A kind of leather dyed with soluble dyes so that it retains the original hide's skin structure and natural characteristics, such as the 'grain' texture on the surface.

Appliqué
/ Elements applied to a bag's surface for decorative purposes. These may include embroidery, beads, sequins, hardware, colored fabric or leather.

Attaché Case
/ A typically boxy, hard-sided, hinged briefcase used for carrying papers and documents.

Backpack
/ A large bag used for carrying items on the back, the backpack was given its name in the 1910's in the USA. Backpacks are particularly popular for outdoor activities, such as camping or hiking.

Bag Bottom
/ A bag's bottom panel, which is usually made of self-fabric or material of the same weight as the side panels.

Baguette Bag
/ A long, narrow handbag which resembles the shape of a French baguette.

Barrel Bag
/ A cylindrical bag with a barrel-shaped compartment.

Beach Bag
/ A large bag designed for carrying items to and from the beach, such as a bathing suit, towel, sunscreen lotion, etc. It can be made of a variety of materials including canvas and straw.

Bermuda Bag
/ A type of bag that was highly popular in the 1980's, characterized by its oval shape, wooden top handles and interchangeable decorative fabric covers.

Basket
/ Typically woven from cane or wire, a basket is a structured container used for holding or carrying various objects or food.

Belt
/ Commonly made from leather or heavy fabrics, a belt is a flexible strap or band designed to be worn around the waist. Belts can be used to hold up trousers or other bottoms, to cinch in loose dresses and coats, or worn purely for decoration and styling.

Belt Bag
/ Also known as a 'waist pack', a belt bag is a type of purse attached to a belt, designed to be worn around the waist. The bag is sometimes detachable from the belt.

Bi-fold Wallet
/ A wallet folded into two halves with a center fold. Banknotes are folded over while cards can be stored vertically or horizontally.

Box Bag
/ A type of hard, boxy shaped handbag.

Briefcase
/ A rectangular case made of leather, manmade materials or plastic, used for holding documents and books. It is carried with a top handle.

Bucket Bag
/ A bag with a rounded base and drawstring cinched opening, thus named due to its bucket-like shape. Its height is usually greater than its width.

Camera Bag
/ A padded bag with specially designed compartments to hold and protect photography equipment, such as cameras and accessories.

Canteen Bag
/ Named after the traditional water bottle used by hikers and soldiers known as a 'canteen', a canteen bag is a stiff, round-shaped bag that usually comes with a shoulder strap.

Canvas
/ Made from either natural or synethetic fibers or a blend of the two, canvas is a versatile, low-cost and durable textile that can be heavy or light in weight.

Carry-on Luggage / Cabin Luggage
/ Bags or cases of the perfect size to be carried on board flights and which would fit in the cabin's overhead storage locker. They come in various forms ranging from totes, suitcases, duffels to backpacks. While most are designed to meet cabin requirements, passengers are advised to check in advance whether their bag's measurements comply with the airline's baggage rules.

Clasp
/ Usually made of metal, a clasp is a fastening device used for attaching a shoulder strap to a bag, or for holding a clutch, wallet or a handbag's flap shut.

Clutch
/ Typically without straps or handles, a clutch is a small handbag designed to be handheld or carried under the arm. Due to its compact size, clutches are usually used for evening occasions to carry minimal essentials such as a phone, credit cards and smaller cosmetic items.

Coin Purse
/ Also known as a change purse, a coin purse is a small bag used for holding loose coins or other tiny items.

Combination Lock
/ A type of locking mechanism that requires the user to key in a sequence of symbols or numbers to unlock the device, instead of using a key like for a regular padlock.

Compartment
/ A large interior section of a bag.

Compression Straps
/ Typically found on backpacks, compression straps are used for compressing and stabilizing loose contents in a bag.

Cosmetic Bag
/ A pouch or case used for carrying cosmetics and toiletries.

Crossbody Bag
/ A smaller bag with a long shoulder strap designed to be worn across the body, keeping the wearer's hands free while commuting.

Daypack
/ A backpack of small or medium size intended for day use. Lighter and more compact, they are suitable for school, short hikes, or for daily errand runs.

Diaper Bag
/ A type of bag designed to carry everything needed to take care of a baby. A diaper bag typically comprises multiple compartments and pockets, while some have extra features such as matching changing pads.

Doctor's Bag
/ Originally used by physicians, traditional doctor's bags were constructed from leather and featured a split handle which opened from the top. Modernized versions come in a variety of different materials and designs, such as multiple pockets and pouches, and may be fastened with a zipper or hook-and-loop closure.

Dopp Kit
/ A travel-friendly toiletry bag for men to store their grooming tools and personal sundries, such as razors, shaving cream, toothbrush and toothpaste, deodorant, combs, shampoo, scissors, cologne, etc.

Drawstring Handbag
/ A bag that is cinched closed by a drawstring or drawcord.

Duffel
/ Alternatively spelt 'duffle', a duffel is a cylindrical bag with top handles and a spacious compartment. duffels are highly versatile and practical, and can be used as cabin luggage, checked baggage, gym bags or sports bags. They sometimes come with extra features such as wheels and shoulder straps.

Dust Cover
/ Also known as a dust bag, a dust cover is a protective cloth drawstring bag used for storing handbags when not in use. Many luxury leather or designer handbags often come with a complimentary dust cover.

East West (or E/W)
/ Describes a bag that is horizontal in shape, with a width greater than its height.

Embossed
/ A type of finishing on leather or faux leather that gives it an imprinted texture or design. Embossed leather and faux leather are often used to imitate and substitute exotic skins such as crocodile and snakeskin.

Envelope Clutch
/ A slim clutch bag with a triangle flap closure, designed to resemble an envelope.

Evening Bag
/ Any style of handbag, such as a clutch, wristlet, or shoulder bag, that is designed to complement more formal attire at special occasions like weddings, cocktail events, dinner parties, date nights, etc.

Expandable Luggage
/ Luggage that can be unzipped and expanded to create more room for storage.

Faux Leather
/ Synthetic materials such as vinyl and PVC that are designed to resemble leather in both look and feel.

Feet
/ Metal or plastic knobs attached to the base of a bag to allow it to stand on its own when not in use. Also called protective feet, they elevate the bag off the ground thus protecting the base from dirt, moisture and scrapes.

Flap Bag
/ A pouch or bag that closes with a folding flap.

Full Grain Leather
/ Leather that has been specially tanned to retain the appearance and visibility of the natural texture, known as 'grain', of the original hide.

Garment Bag
/ A bag used for protecting garments, in particular suits and dresses, during transit or travel. Extra features may include shoe pockets and toiletry pockets.

Gig Bag / Guitar Bag
/ A bag constructed with protective padding and soft sides, designed to store, protect and carry musical instruments, especially guitars or bass guitars.

Gladstone Bag
/ Named after four-time Prime Minister of Great Britain, William Ewart Gladstone, the Gladstone bag is a boxy briefcase-like travel bag. Traditionally made from stiff leather and often fitted with lanyard belts, it is constructed with a hinged rigid frame which opens and closes the bag.

Golf Bag
/ A bag designed to hold golfing equipment. It is normally lighter in weight as it is intended to be carried from hole to hole across the golf course.

Grain
/ Refers to the pattern on the surface of leather, which varies depending on the animal it originated from.

Handbag
/ A bag which is larger than a purse, designed for women to hold their personal items and daily essentials.

Hardside Luggage
/ A suitcase constructed from harder and more durable materials, such as aluminum, ABS, polycarbonate, polypropylene, etc.

Hobo Bag
/ A slouchy shaped shoulder bag with a long, usually flat shoulder strap and a scooped center.

It Bag
/ A colloquial term used in the 1990's to 2000's by the fashion industry to describe a sought-after and best-selling designer handbag from popular high-fashion brands such as Chanel, Hermès and Fendi.

Kiss Lock Handbag
/ A handbag fastened by a kiss lock clasp — a type of framed closure which snaps shut with two spherical knobs.

Knapsack
/ Before the mid 20th century, 'knapsack' was the common

Laptop Bag / A bag designed with padded compartments for holding and protecting a laptop computer.

Lining / The layer of material or fabric used for lining a bag's interior for protection or aesthetic purposes.

Long Wallet / A wallet which is longer in shape and can hold banknotes flat and uncreased. Also known as continental wallets, long wallets are fastened by a zipper, leather rein or snap button strap, and commonly feature a coin purse.

Luggage Handle Wrap / A band or piece of material that wraps around the luggage handle to offer a more comfortable grip and make it easier to spot at baggage claim.

Luggage Tag / A tag attached to luggage for identification purposes.

Medicine Bag / A small pouch traditionally worn by native American shamans to hold items for spiritual healing. It is typically made of leather or suede and decorated with fringes or tribal embroidery.

Messenger Bag / A large and usually horizontal crossbody bag with a long, adjustable shoulder strap and a flap cover. It is named after the style of bags traditionally carried by mail couriers.

Minaudière / Typically richly embellished with beads or crystals, a minaudière is a small hard-cased clutch or evening bag suitable for grand and formal occasions.

Money Belt / A pouch attached to a belt designed to be worn underneath clothing to safeguard personal belongings and valuables from pickpockets, especially when traveling. Compact and usually flat, it can hold money, credit cards and travel documents.

Muff Bag / A combination of a muff and a handbag. A muff bag features a tubular fur-lined case to keep both hands warm in the cold weather.

Name Plate / A leather or metal plaque which displays the handbag's brand name or logo. It is can be sewn or riveted to either the exterior or interior of the bag.

Nap / Napped / The finely bristled structure found on the surface of nubuck leather and suede which gives a soft, fuzzy handfeel.

North South (or N/S) / Describes a bag that is vertical in shape, with a height greater than its width.

Nubuck / A type of soft aniline leather which has been brushed, buffed or sanded to create a suede-like texture. Due to its napped surface, it is easily stained even after being treated with stain protection.

Nylon / Nylon is regarded as the strongest synthetic textile, known for its high resistance to abrasion and stains. It is commonly used in tote bags due to its durable nature.

One Strap Bookbag / A single-strapped backpack meant to be carried on one shoulder.

Open Pocket / A pocket that is open at the top and does not have a fastening or closure.

Packing Cube / A cuboid-shaped zipper case designed for storing and protecting garments, shoes and other items when traveling. Packing cubes keep items tidy and well-organized within a suitcase and effectively prevent clothing from getting creased.

Padlock / Opened and locked with a key, a padlock is a portable locking device with a pivotable shackle which can be inserted through an opening on a gate, locker door, suitcase, etc., to protect the valuables within.

Patent Leather / A type of leather with a glossy, high-shine finish.

Portfolio Bag / A large flat case used by artists, designers and students to carry items such as drawings, paper or photographs. It prevents the content within from getting folded or creased.

Purse Hook / Purse Hanger / A device used for temporarily suspending your handbag from a table to prevent theft and to protect it from dust and dirt on the floor. It features a flat pad which rests on the tabletop, and a hook for holding the handbag.

Quilted Handbag / A handbag made from quilted fabric with a decorative topstitched pattern.

Randoseru / A distinct type of backpack used by Japanese elementary school students. Made from stitched sturdy leather or synthetic leather, it typically features a flap cover and a boxy, firm-sided construction, designed to be durable as schoolchildren usually use the same bag for six years. The name is a loanword which originated from the Dutch word 'ransel', which means 'backpack'.

Rivet / A metal pin that is used for binding two sheets of material, such as leather or metal, together or purely for decoration. Flat and larger on one end (the head), it has a cylindrical shaft at the other end which is inserted through the material then hammered to form a flat head, as a result keeping the material secured in place.

Rucksack / An alternative name for 'backpack' mainly used in the UK and amongst Western military. The name was borrowed from the Germany words 'der rücken', which means 'the back of the body', and 'sack', which means 'bag'.

Saddle Bag / The most traditional form of the saddle bag consists of two large bags or pouches which hang on either side of a saddle on the hips of a horse. In cycling, saddle bags could be attached under the seat of a motorcycle or bicycle. Nowadays, it also refers to a small horseshoe-shaped crossbody bag with a flap cover.

Satchel / Traditionally used by school children to carry books, a satchel is a rectangular leather bag featuring a flap cover and a long shoulder strap.

Shopper / A rectangular tote suitable for shopping.

Shoulder Bag / Refers to all types of bags which can be carried across the shoulder with a strap.

Shoulder Strap / A length of fabric or other flexible materials designed to suspend a bag, allowing it to be worn over the shoulder, either slung over one shoulder or across the body. Shoulder straps can be made from leather, vinyl, textile, rubber or a variety of other materials.

Sporran / A small pouch worn around the waist to serve as a pocket for a kilt, a kind of traditional male Scottish highland costume which does not have pockets.

Straw Bags / A handbag woven or knitted from plant fibers, such as straw, rattan, raffia, seagrass, jute, willow, corn husk, etc.

Suede / A type of leather with a napped surface texture and a velvety, fuzzy handfeel. Synthetic suede is also commonly used as a substitute for genuine suede.

Suitcase / Designed for holding items of clothing and other personal belongings when traveling, a suitcase is typically boxy in shape, with a handle and a hinged lid which is fastened with a zipper or a snap lock.

Tassel / A bundle of leather fringes, threads or cords attached to a cylindrical cap used for decoration.

Toiletry Kit / A travel-friendly bag used for storing toiletries and personal sundries. Variations include hanging cases, cosmetic bags, countertop kits, manicure sets, shave kits, etc.

Top Grain Leather / Leather is always divided into multiple layers before use, amongst which top grain leather is the topmost layer.

Top Handle / A handle attached to the top of bag allowing it to be carried by hand.

Top Zip Bag / A bag whose compartment can be closed by a zipper at the top.

Tote / A large bag typically with an unfastened open-top compartment and parallel double top handles.

Tri-fold Wallet / A wallet folded into three sections with two folds. Cards are usually stored vertically in a tri-fold wallet.

Trunk / Alternatively known as a travel trunk, a trunk is a boxy shaped container designed to hold items of clothing and other personal belongings when traveling. Trunks can come in different sizes, varying from 30-36 inches in length, 16-22 inches in width and various heights.

TSA Lock / A TSA lock is specially designed for TSA baggage checks and can be opened by special tools by the authority without damaging the lock. TSA stands for Transport Security Adminstration, an agency of the U.S. Department of Homeland Security which has the authority to screen every passenger's baggage before it can board an aircraft. At their discretion, TSA may choose to open a passenger's checked baggage for closer inspection. If a suitcase selected for inspection uses a regular lock instead of a TSA lock, it will be destroyed by TSA in order to gain access.

Waist Pack / Bum Bag / A type of bag worn around the waist to hold smaller objects and minimal essentials. It is especially useful as it keeps the wearer hands-free during travel, jogging or hiking.

Wallet / A small, flat case used for holding money, credit cards, personal identification documents, business cards, etc. Typically made from leather or textile, wallets come in both foldable and non-folded variations and are usually compact enough to fit in the pocket. Women's wallets are commonly called 'purse' in British English, while Americans often refer to the folded wallet as a 'billfold'.

Weekender / Holdall / Generally with a rectangular base, a weekender or holdall is a large leather or fabric bag fastened with a top zipper. It is usually spacious enough to hold personal contents for a short weekend trip.

Wristlet / A wallet or clutch with a loop-shaped wristlet strap designed to be worn around the wrist.

Zipper Pull / The tab attached to the slider of a zipper which can be used to pull the zipper open.

PART VII

BAG TEMPLATES

Pouch
P. 60

Clutch
P. 61

Envelope Clutch
P. 62

Minaudière
P. 63

Kiss Lock Clutch
P. 64

Wristlet
P. 65

Box Bag
P. 66

Doctor's Bag
P. 67

Boston Bag
P. 68

Gladstone Bag
P. 69

Handheld Handbag
- Single Handle
P. 70

Handheld Handbag
- Double Handle
P. 71

Handheld Handbag
- Accordion Handbag
P. 72

Handheld Handbag
- Trapeze Handbag
P. 73

Handheld Handbag
- Half Moon Handbag
P. 74

Handheld Handbag
- Ruffle Handbag
P. 75

Baguette Bag
P. 76

Hobo Bag
P. 77

**Straw Bag /
Beach Bag / Kenya Bag**
P. 78

Shopper Bag
- Double Handle
P. 79

Shopper Bag
- Cut-out Handle
P. 80

Tote Bag
- Zippered Top
P. 81

Tote Bag
- Open Top
P. 82

Fringe Bag
P. 83

Bucket Bag
P. 84

Accordion Handbag
P. 85

Canteen Bag
P. 86

Saddle Bag
P. 87

Saddle Bag
- with Tassel
P. 88

Satchel
P. 89

**Quilted Sling /
Crossbody Bag**
P. 90

Lady Camera Bag
P. 91

**One Strap Bookbag /
One Shoulder Backpack /
Sling Backpack**
P. 92

Belt Bag
P. 93

Waist Pack / Bum Bag
P. 94

Day Pack
P. 95

Backpack
P. 96

Drawstring Backpack
P. 97

Knapsack
P. 98

Rucksack
P. 99

Satchel Backpack
P. 100

**Security Pouch /
Small Traveling Pouch**
P. 101

Wash Bag / Cosmetic Bag
P. 102

Weekender
P. 103

Sports Duffel Bag
P. 104

Barrel Bag / Holdall
P. 105

Bowling Bag
P. 106

Bowling Bag
- as Fashion Item
P. 107

**Messenger Bag /
Courier Bag**
P. 108

Field Bag
P. 109

Computer / Laptop Bag
P. 110

Camera Bag
P. 111

Hiking Backpack
P. 112

Golf Bag
P. 113

Hardside Luggage
P. 114

Softside Luggage
- in Cabin Luggage Size
P. 116

Continental / Long Wallet
P. 118

Zip-around Wallet
P. 119

Bi-fold Wallet
P. 120

Key Case
P. 121

POUCH

A small bag which is usually fastened by a top zipper closure. It can be handheld as a clutch or used to hold smaller items within a larger handbag. Its history dates back to the medieval times, when it was designed in the form of drawstring pouches.

Top View

Bottom View

Side View

Back View

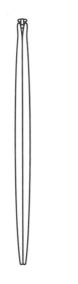

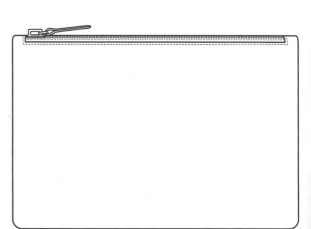

¾ Front View

CLUTCH

Typically without straps or handles, a clutch is a small handbag designed to be handheld or carried under the arm. Due to its compact size, clutches are usually used for evening occasions to carry minimal essentials such as a phone, credit cards and smaller cosmetic items.

Top View

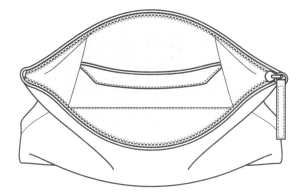

Bottom View

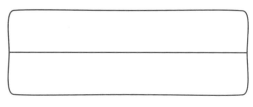

Side View

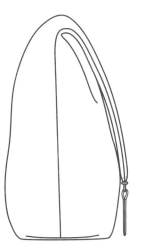

Back View

¾ Front View

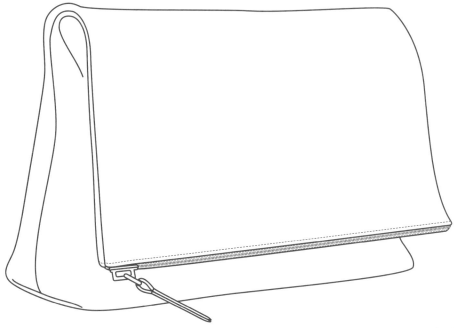

ENVELOPE CLUTCH

A slim clutch bag with a triangle flap closure, designed to resemble an envelope. It is a better choice for people who do not prefer zipper closures.

Top View

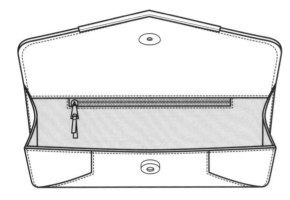

Bottom View

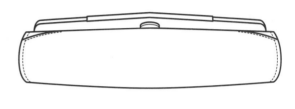

Side View

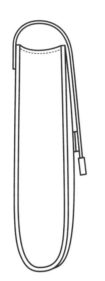

Back View

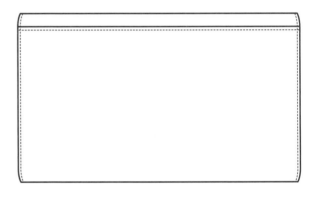

¾ Front View

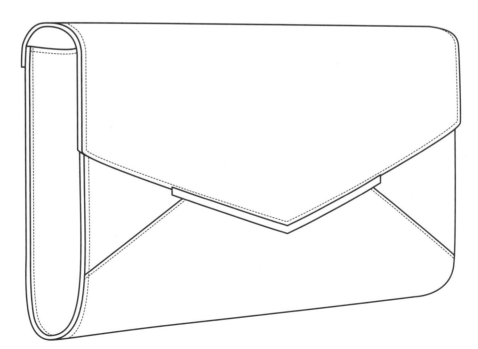

MINAUDIÈRE

Typically richly embellished with beads or crystals, a minaudière is a small hard-cased clutch or evening bag suitable for grand and formal occasions.

The world's first minaudière was invented by luxury jeweler Van Cleef & Arpels in 1930. It was inspired by the metal cigarette case used by Florence Gould, an American socialite and patron of the arts, to carry her belongings.

op View

Bottom View

de View

Back View

Front View

KISS LOCK CLUTCH

A handbag fastened by a kiss lock clasp — a type of framed closure which snaps shut with two spherical knobs.

Top View

Bottom View

Side View

Back View

¾ Front View

WRISTLET

A wallet or clutch with a loop-shaped wristlet strap designed to be worn around the wrist.
Wristlets are considered more convenient than clutch bags as they can be looped around the wrist to free up your hands, whereas clutches need to be handheld at all times.

Top View

Bottom View

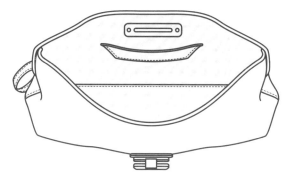

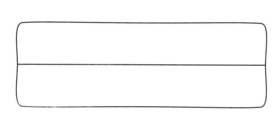

Side View

Back View

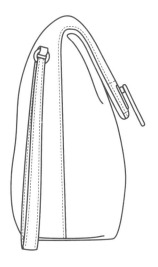

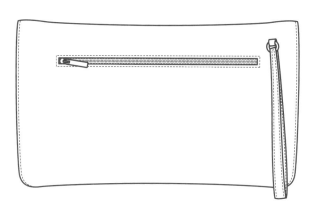

¾ Front View

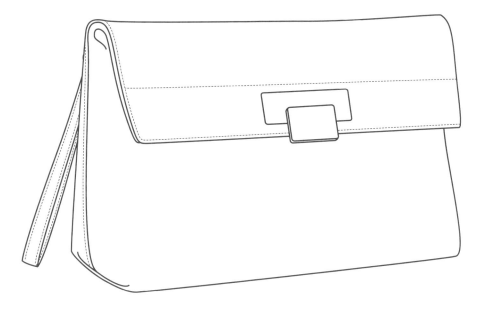

BOX BAG

A type of hard, boxy shaped handbag. With a more defined structure, box bags are a sleeker and sturdier alternative to traditional handbags, which are typically soft and more casual.

Top View

Bottom View

Side View

Back View

¾ Front View

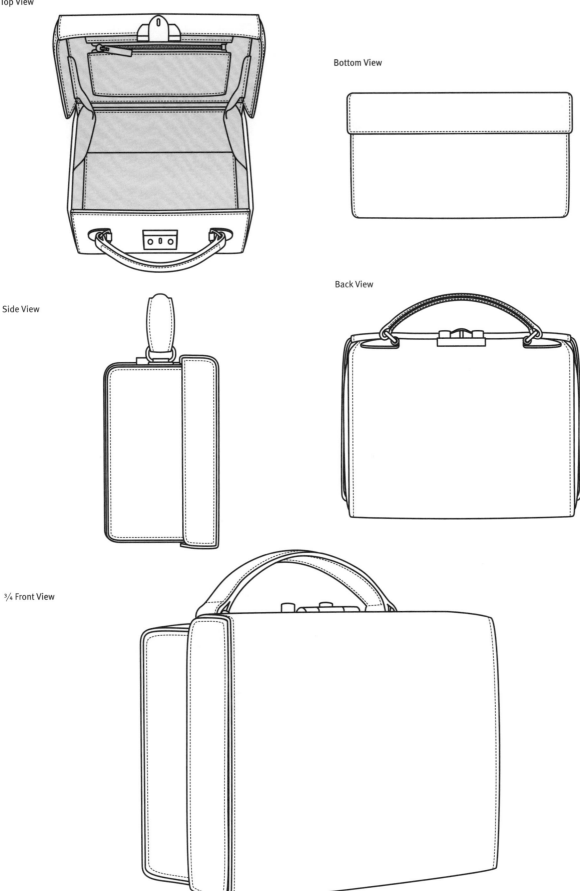

DOCTOR'S BAG

Originally used by physicians, traditional doctor's bags were constructed from leather and featured a split handle which opened from the top. Modernized versions come in a variety of different materials and designs, such as multiple pockets and pouches, and may be fastened with a zipper or hook-and-loop closure.

Top View

Bottom View

Side View

Back View

¾ Front View

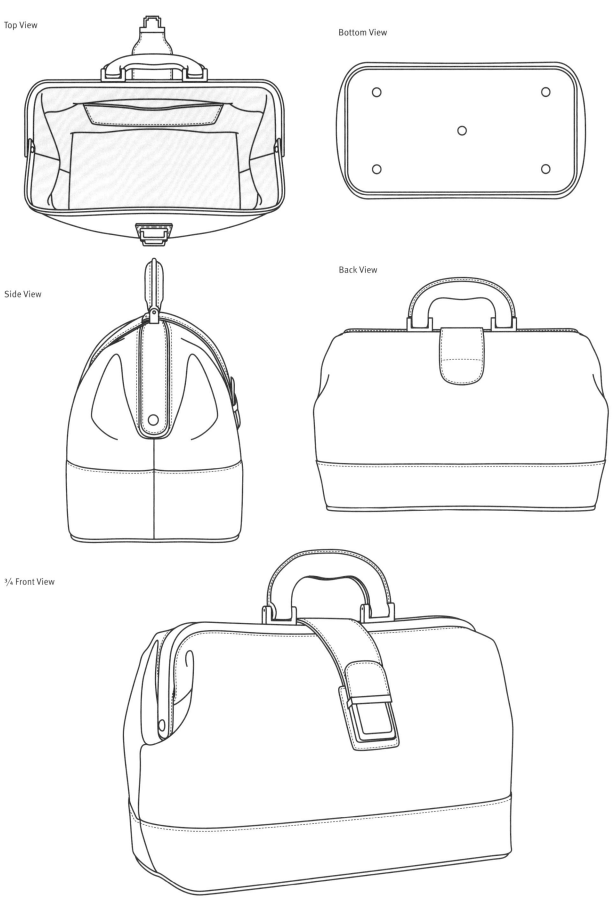

BOSTON BAG

A barrel-shaped bag with a top zipper closure and handheld with two top handles.

Top View

Bottom View

Back View

Side View

¾ Front View

GLADSTONE BAG

Named after four-time Prime Minister of Great Britain, William Ewart Gladstone, the Gladstone bag is a boxy briefcase-like travel bag. Traditionally made from stiff leather and often fitted with lanyard belts, it is constructed with a hinged rigid frame which opens and closes the bag.

Top View

Bottom View

Side View

Back View

¾ Front View

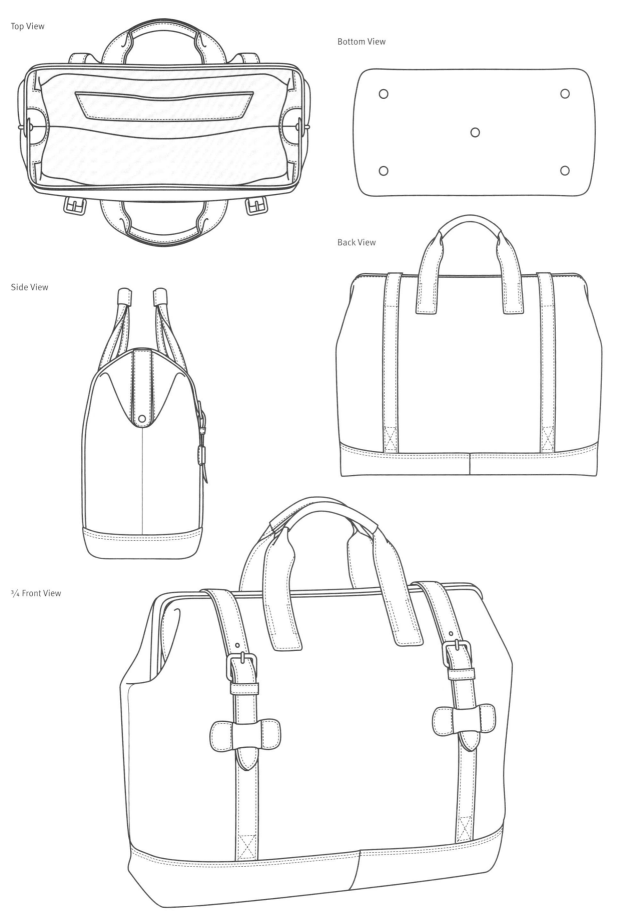

HANDHELD HANDBAG
SINGLE HANDLE

A bag which is larger than a purse, designed for women to hold their personal items and daily essentials.
The Kelly bag from Hermès was one of the first ever 'It Bags'. Hailed as a symbol of status, the bag got its name when Grace Kelly, the Princess of Monaco, was spotted using the handbag to shield her baby bump from the paparazzi. After the photo was published, the bag quickly received attention and gained popularity.

Top View

Back View

Bottom View

¾ Front View

Side View

HANDHELD
HANDBAG
DOUBLE HANDLE

A bag which is larger than a purse, designed for women to hold their personal items and daily essentials.
The 'First' bag by Balenciaga was introduced in June 2000 by then creative director Nicolas Ghesquière. It was succeeded eighteen months later by the iconic City bag, the oft-copied moto-chic top handle bag which was favoured even by style icons such as Kate Moss and Sienna Miller. The diagram below shows a style similar to Balenciaga's City bag.

Top View

Bottom View

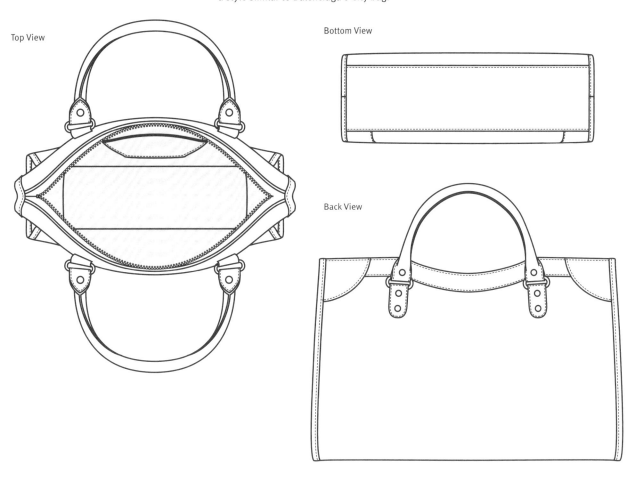

Back View

¾ Front View

Side View

HANDHELD HANDBAG
ACCORDION STYLE

A bag which is larger than a purse, designed for women to hold their personal items and daily essentials.

Purses were initially used by early modern Europeans, both men and women, for carrying coins. Made of leather or soft fabric, they were always very small in size. During the Industrial Revolution in England, increased railway travel led to the demand for larger-sized handbags as purses were too small and the materials were not durable enough for the journey.

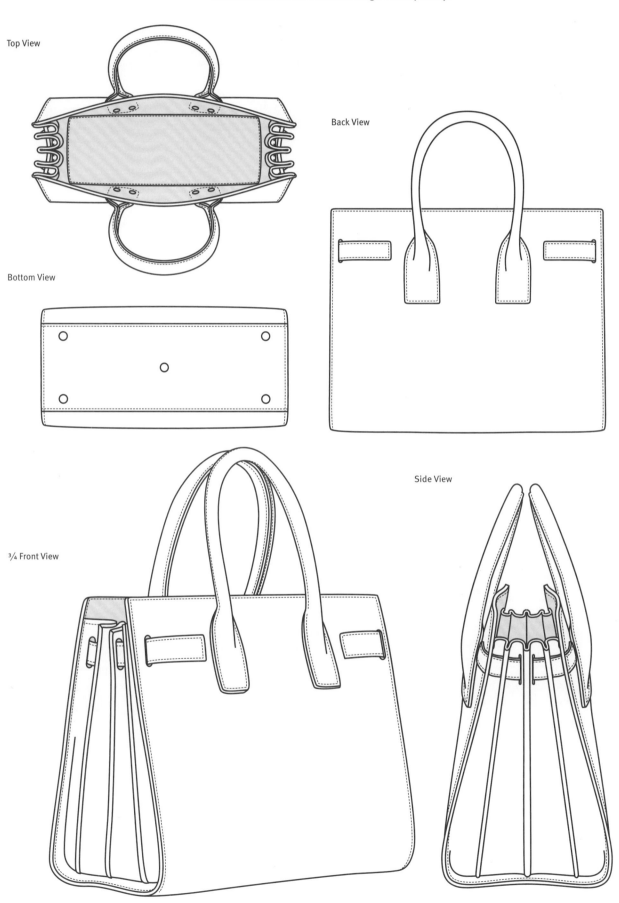

Top View

Back View

Bottom View

¾ Front View

Side View

HANDHELD HANDBAG

TRAPEZE HANDBAG

A bag which is larger than a purse, designed for women to hold their personal items and daily essentials.

The trapeze handbag's distinctive trapezoid shape gives it a more refined, architectural appeal. Luxury French fashion house Céline made this style famous with its highly sought-after Trapeze bag, which features a flap cover, single top handle and signature winged sides.

Top View

Bottom View

Back View

Side View

¾ Front View

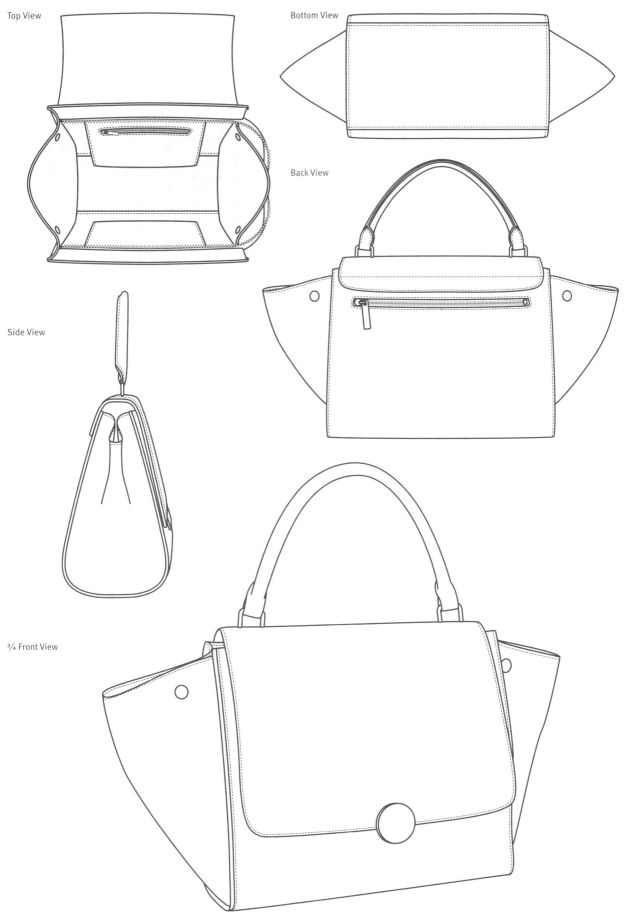

HANDHELD HANDBAG
HALF MOON HANDBAG

A bag which is larger than a purse, designed for women to hold their personal items and daily essentials.
A half-moon shaped handbag in which two corners are rounded off for a softer appearance.

Top View

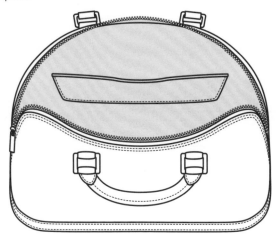

Back View

Bottom View

¾ Front View

Side View

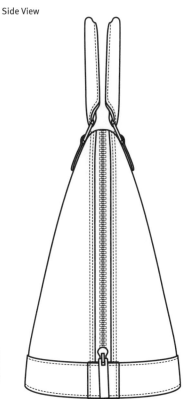

HANDHELD HANDBAG
RUFFLE HANDBAG

A bag which is larger than a purse, designed for women to hold their personal items and daily essentials.
Prada's Gaufre Tote is one of the most iconic ruffle handbags. It gave Prada's classic elegance a fun and youthful twist.

Top View

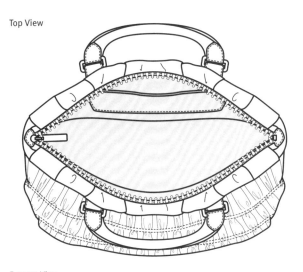

Bottom View

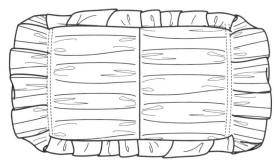

Back View

¾ Front View

Side View

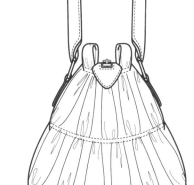

BAGUETTE BAG

A long, narrow handbag which resembles the shape of a French baguette. One of the most iconic baguette handbags in history is the Fendi Baguette, which achieved It-bag status after it was featured in the wildly popular American TV comedy Sex and the City. It was used by Carrie Bradshaw, the protagonist played by Sarah Jessica Parker, throughout the entire series.

Top View

Back View

Bottom View

¾ Front View

Side View

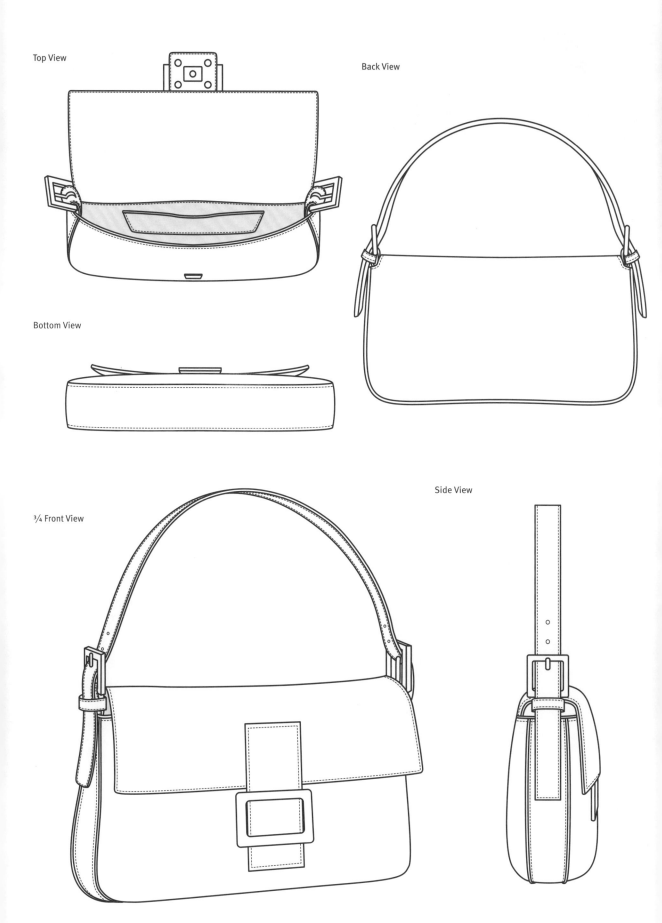

HOBO BAG

A slouchy shaped shoulder bag with a long, usually flat shoulder strap and a scooped center. Gucci's Jackie bag is one of the most well-known hobo bags in fashion history. It was renamed after Jackie Kennedy in around 1961, as the trend-setting First Lady of the United States was often spotted carrying the bag. The original style was designed as a unisex carryall. Subsequently, Tom Ford relaunched the bag in 1999, while creative director Frida Giannini relaunched it again in 2009 as the 'New Jackie'.

Top View

Back View

Bottom View

¾ Front View

Side View

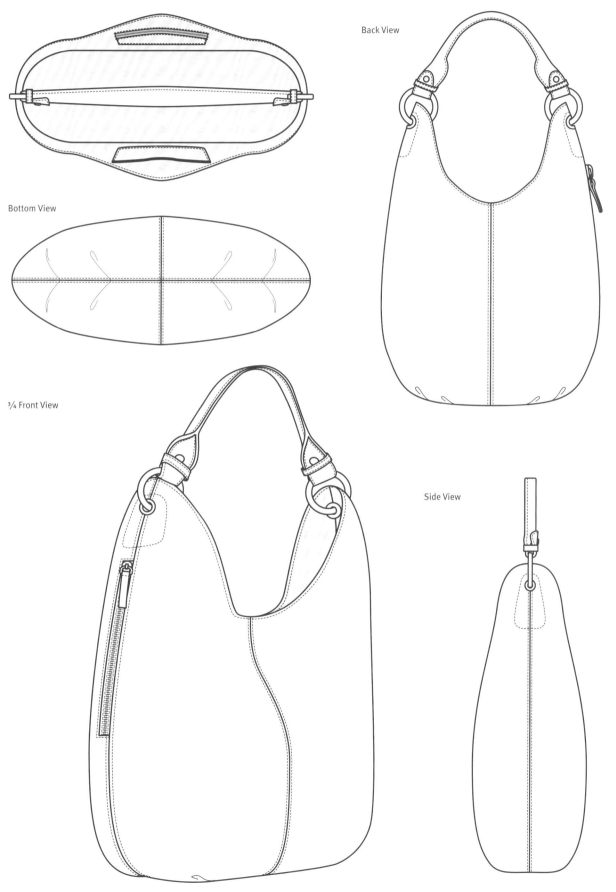

STRAW/ BEACH / KENYA BAG

A large bag designed for carrying items to and from the beach, such as a bathing suit, towel, sunscreen lotion, etc. It can be made of a variety of materials including canvas and straw.

Top View

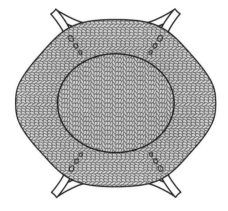

Back View

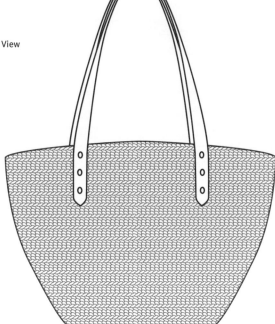

Bottom View

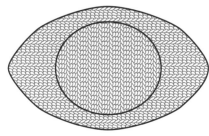

¾ Front View

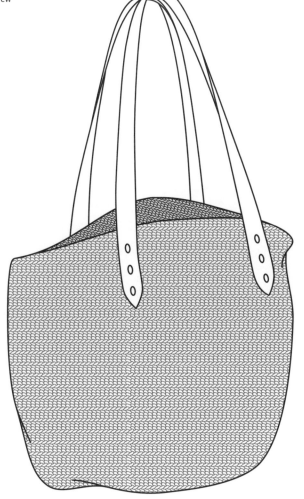

Side View

SHOPPER BAG
DOUBLE HANDLE

A rectangular tote suitable for shopping. A cross between a tote and a box bag, it offers more room to hold your personal belongings and shopping.

Top View

Back View

Bottom View

¾ Front View

Side View

SHOPPER BAG
CUT-OUT HANDLE

A rectangular tote suitable for shopping. A cross between a tote and a box bag, it offers more room to hold your personal belongings and shopping. The cut-out handles are a better alternative for people who do not prefer shoulder straps or top handles.

Top View

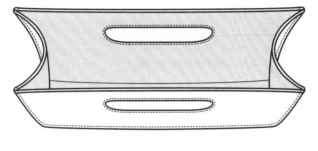

Back View

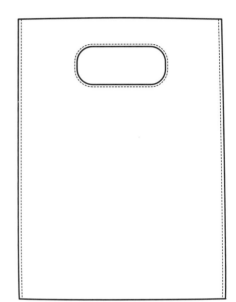

Bottom View

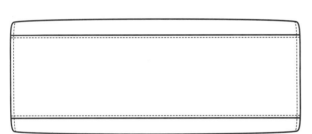

¾ Front View

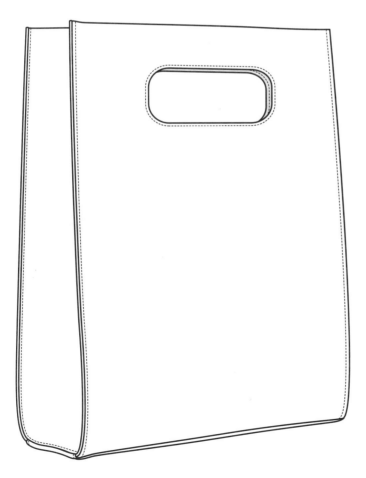

Side View

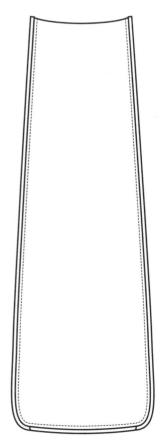

TOTE BAG
ZIPPERED TOP

A large bag typically with an unfastened open-top compartment and parallel double top handles. Longchamp's Le Pliage is one of the most signature totes ever. A foldable design made of water-resistant nylon, it was an instant success since its launch and continues to be the brand's most iconic and best-selling bag to date.

Top View

Back View

Bottom View

¾ Front View

Side View

TOTE BAG
OPEN TOP

A large bag typically with an unfastened open-top compartment and parallel double top handles. A lot of the afforable or free totes nowadays are made from eco-friendly materials, such as recycled matter, minimally processed natural fibers, by-products of organic material refinement processes, etc.

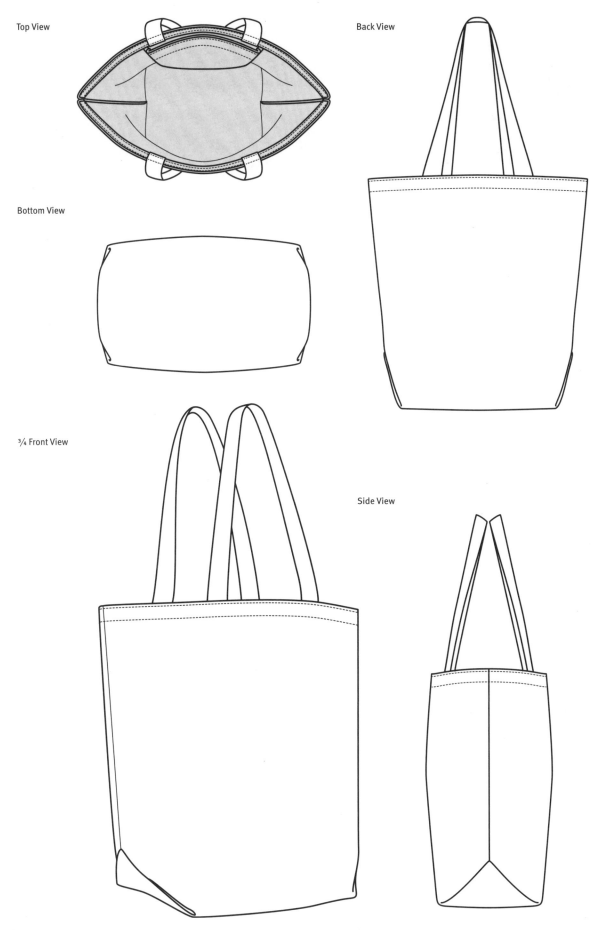

Top View

Back View

Bottom View

¾ Front View

Side View

FRINGE BAG

The fringe bag is an iconic design that encapsulates the 70's bohemian spirit, a recurring trend that is constantly on the style radar. With eye-catching leather or suede fringing which sways with the wearer's movement, it is a fun and playful choice for those who adore the boho or hippie style.

Top View

Bottom View

Back View

¾ Front View

Side View

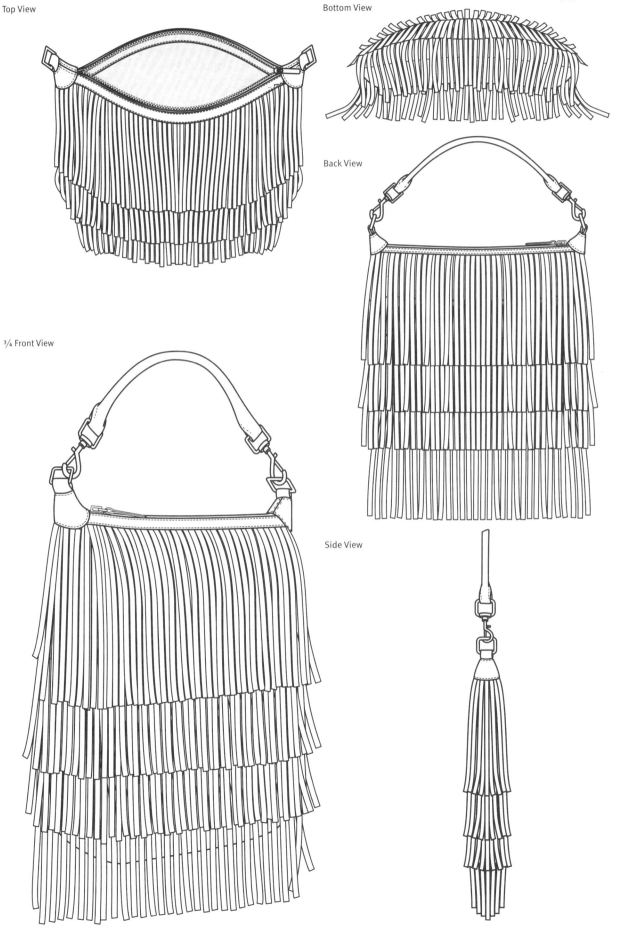

BUCKET BAG

A bag with a rounded base and drawstring cinched opening, thus named due to its bucket-like shape. Its height is usually greater than its width.

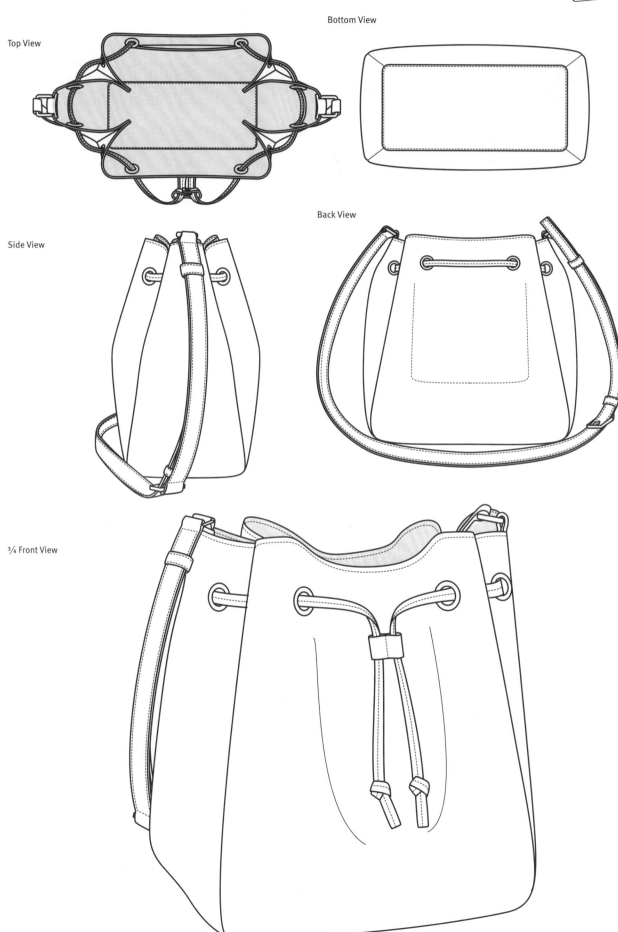

Top View

Bottom View

Side View

Back View

¾ Front View

ACCORDION HANDBAG

A handbag or briefcase with a compartment that folds open like accordion bellows.

Top View

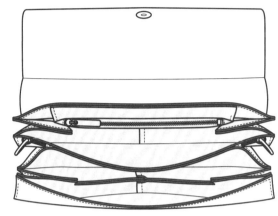

Bottom View

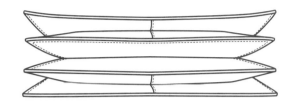

Side View

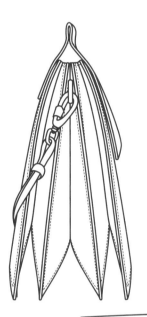

Back View

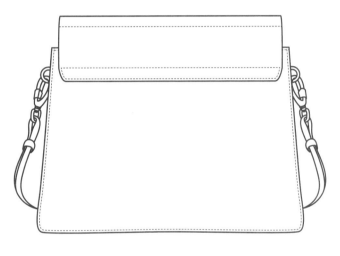

¾ Front View

CANTEEN BAG

Named after the traditional water bottle used by hikers and soldiers known as a 'canteen', a canteen bag is a stiff, round-shaped bag that usually comes with a shoulder strap.

Top View

Bottom View

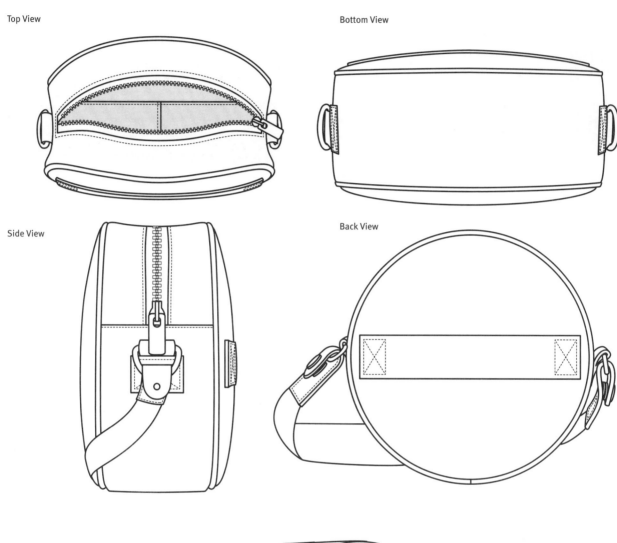

Side View

Back View

¾ Front View

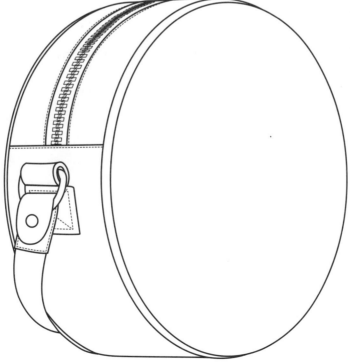

SADDLE BAG

The most traditional form of the saddle bag consists of two large bags or pouches which hang on either side of a saddle on the hips of a horse. In cycling, saddle bags could be attached under the seat of a motorcycle or bicycle. Nowadays, it also refers to a small horseshoe-shaped crossbody bag with a flap cover.

Top View

Bottom View

Side View

Back View

¾ Front View

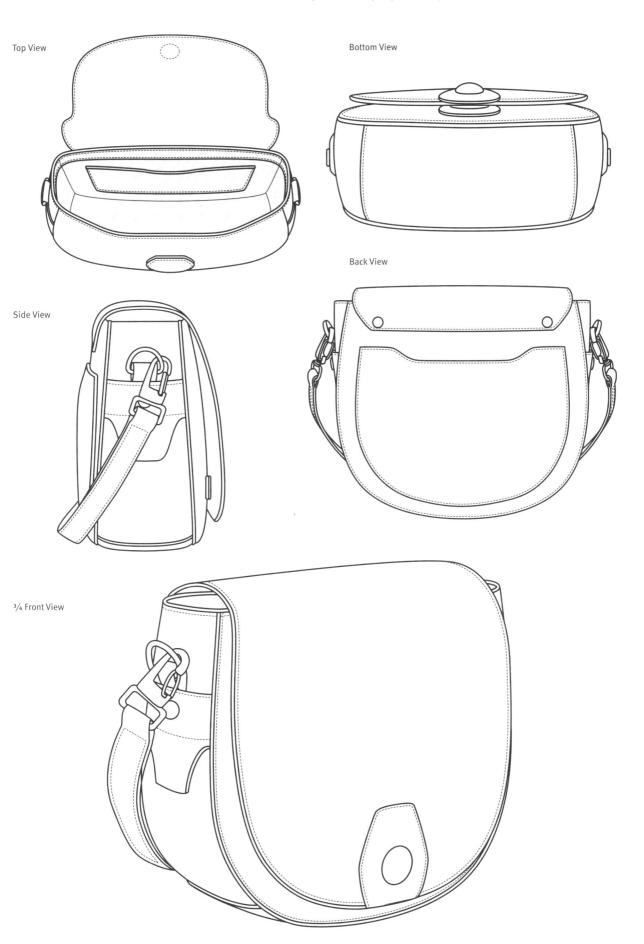

SADDLE BAG
WITH TASSEL

The most traditional form of the saddle bag consists of two large bags or pouches which hang on either side of a saddle on the hips of a horse. In cycling, saddle bags could be attached under the seat of a motorcycle or bicycle. Nowadays, it also refers to a small horseshoe-shaped crossbody bag with a flap cover.

SATCHEL

Traditionally used by school children to carry books, a satchel is a rectangular leather bag featuring a flap cover and a long shoulder strap.
The Cambridge Satchel Company is one of the most internationally renowned satchel manufacturers.

Top View

Bottom View

Side View

Back View

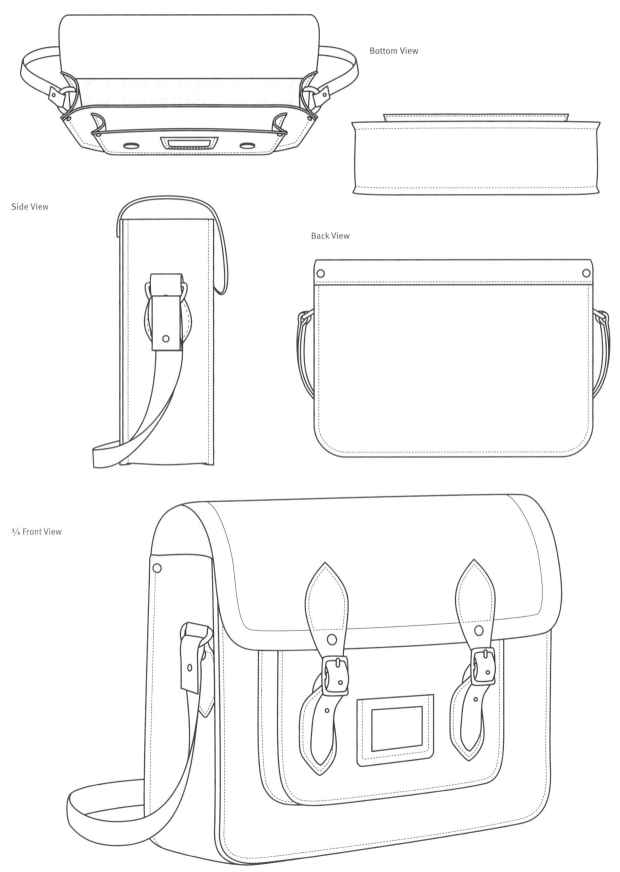

¾ Front View

QUILTED SLING / CROSSBODY BAG

A handbag made from quilted fabric with a decorative topstitched pattern.

Name after its creation date February 1955, Chanel's 2.55 is one of the most legendary quilted bags in history. The iconic design is made of luxurious quilted leather and features a flap cover and chain handles. It is said that the burgundy lining represents the color of the uniform of the convent school Coco Chanel attended, while rumors have it that the inner zipper pocket was where she stashed her love letters.

Top View

Bottom View

Side View

Back View

¾ Front View

LADY CAMERA BAG

In comparison to functional camera bags which are larger and bulkier, trend-conscious ladies prefer smaller camera bags which are just the right size for compact cameras.

Top View

Bottom View

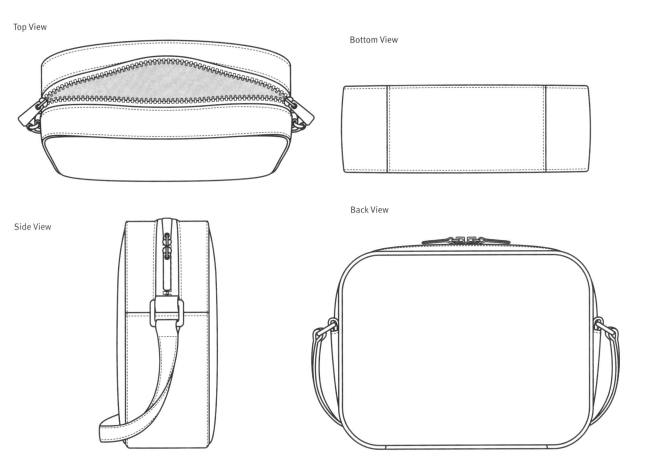

Side View

Back View

¾ Front View

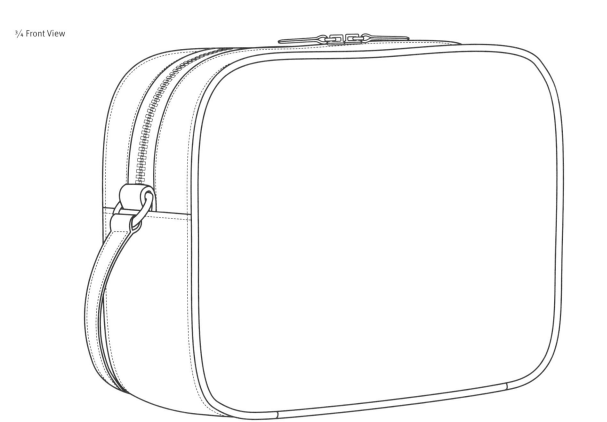

ONE STRAP BOOKBAG
/ ONE SHOULDER BACKPACK / SLING BACKPACK

A single-strapped backpack meant to be carried on one shoulder. Some people dislike backpacks as their straps tend to slip off the shoulders easily. This problem can be solved by using a one shoulder backpack instead, as the single strap keeps the bag better secured across the body.

Inside View

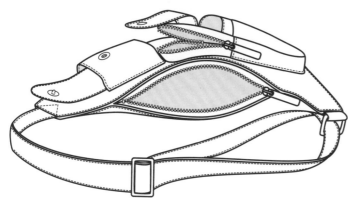

Back View

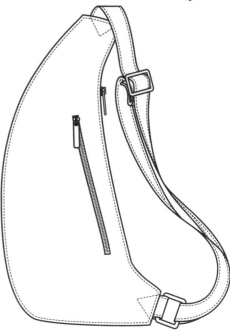

¾ Front View

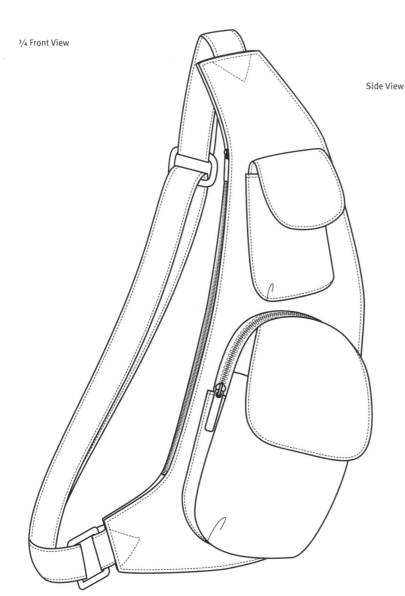

Side View

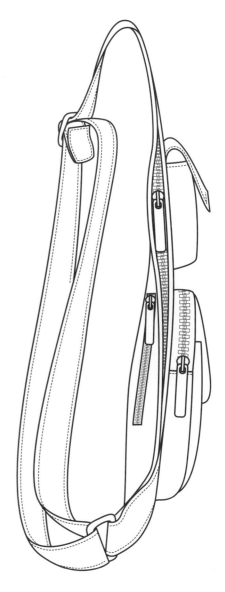

BELT BAG

Also known as a 'waist pack', a belt bag is a type of purse attached to a belt, designed to be worn around the waist. The bag is sometimes detachable from the belt.

Top View

Side View

Bottom View

Back View

3/4 Front View

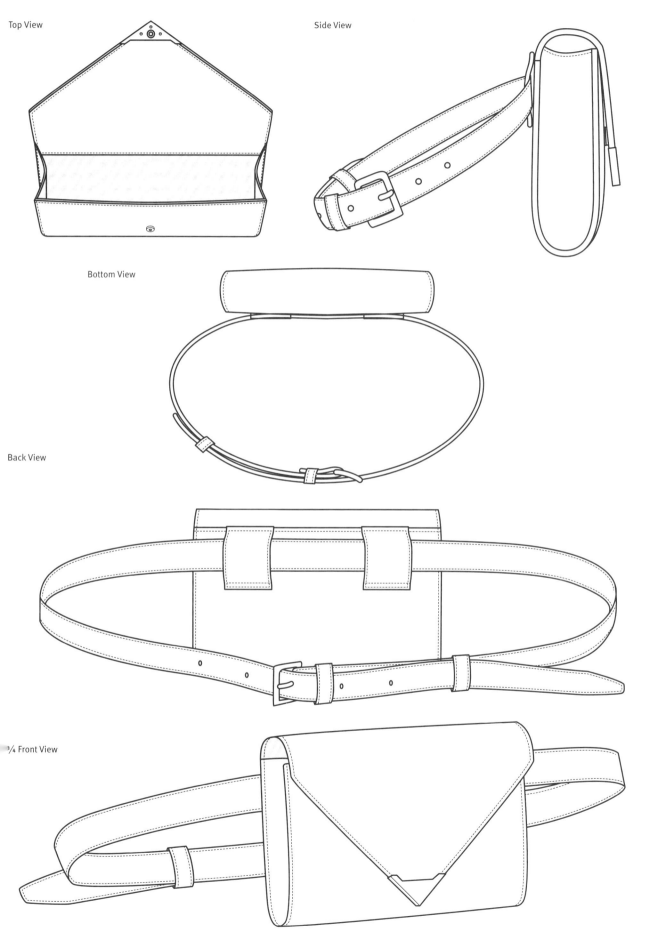

WAIST PACK
/ BUM BAG

A type of bag worn around the waist to hold smaller objects and minimal essentials. It is especially useful as it keeps the wearer hands-free during travel, jogging or hiking.

Top View

Bottom View

Side View

Back View

¾ Front View

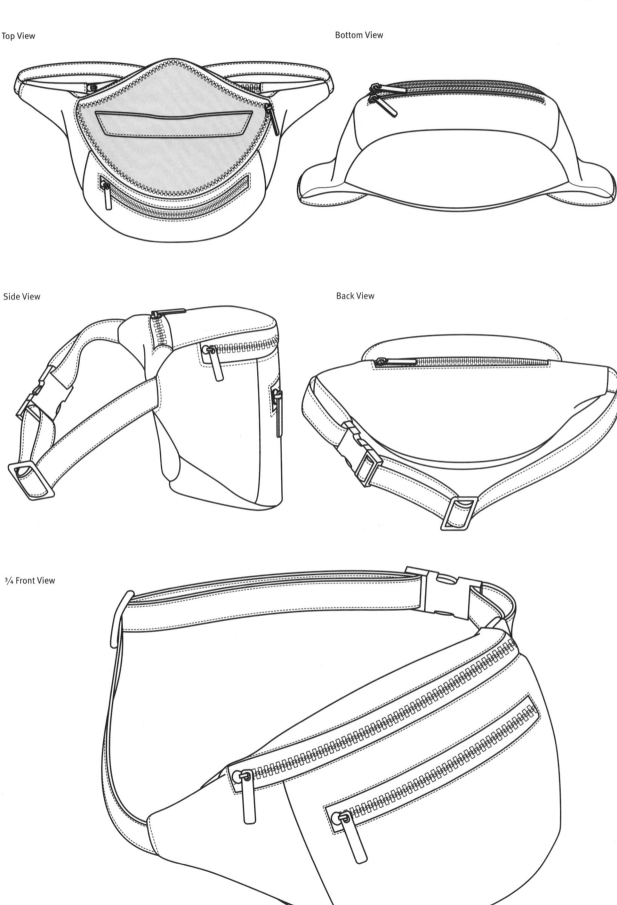

DAY PACK

A backpack of small or medium size intended for day use. Lighter and more compact, they are suitable for school, short hikes, or for daily errand runs.

Top View

Bottom View

Back View

¾ Front View

Side View

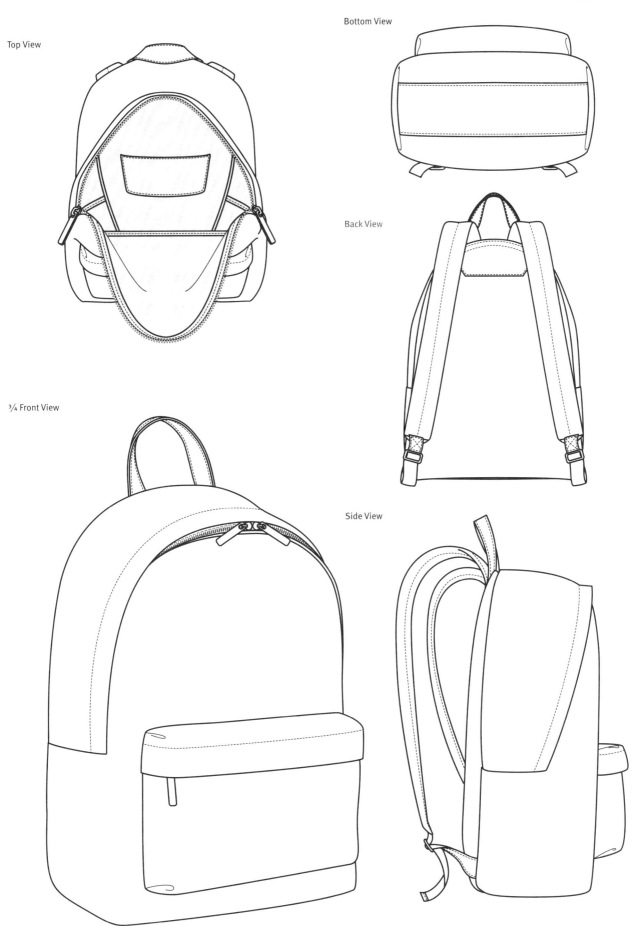

BACKPACK

A large bag used for carrying items on the back, the backpack was given its name in the 1910's in the USA. Backpacks are particularly popular for outdoor activities, such as camping or hiking.

Top View

Bottom View

Back View

¾ Front View

Side View

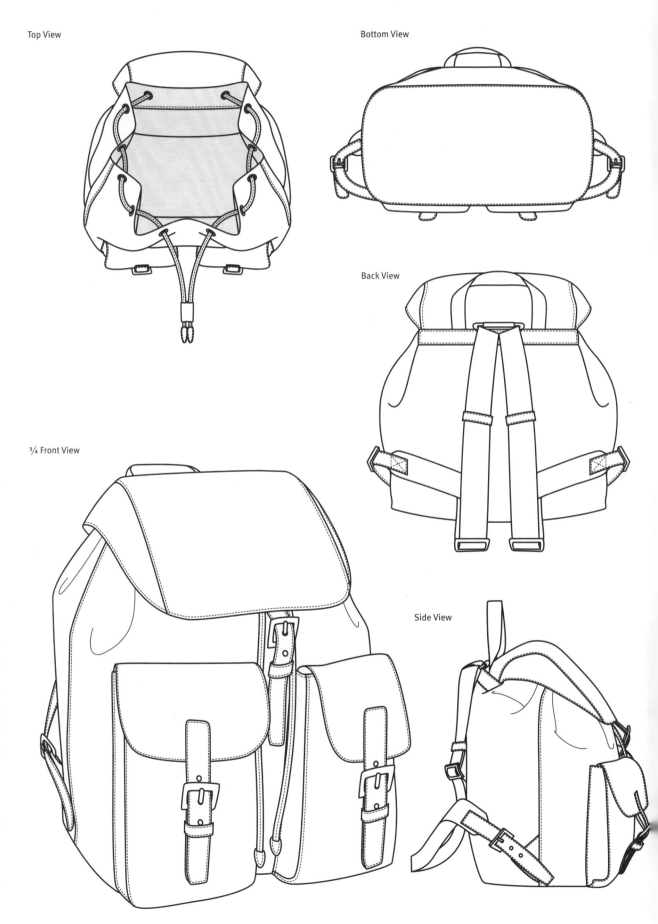

DRAWSTRING BACKPACK

A bag that is cinched closed by a drawstring or drawcord. Drawstring backpacks come in a wide variety of materials, such as canvas, nylon, leather, etc. They are particularly popular amongst young people due to the simple structure and typically more affordable price.

Top View

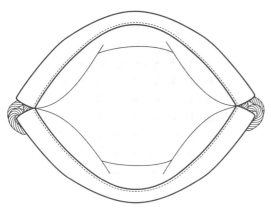

Back View

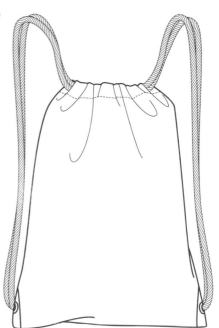

Bottom View

¾ Front View

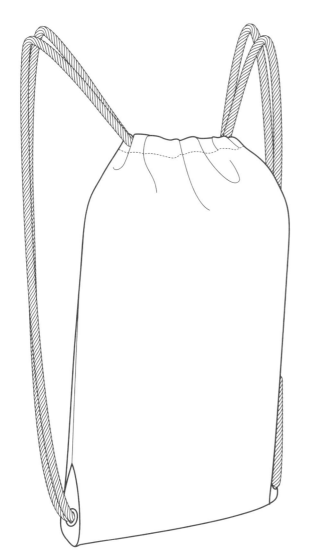

Side View

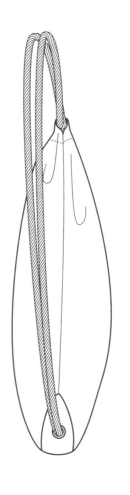

KNAPSACK

Before the mid 20th century, 'knapsack' was the common name for a backpack or rucksack. Made from canvas or leather, it is designed for carrying articles on the back.

Top View

Bottom View

Back View

¾ Front View

Side View

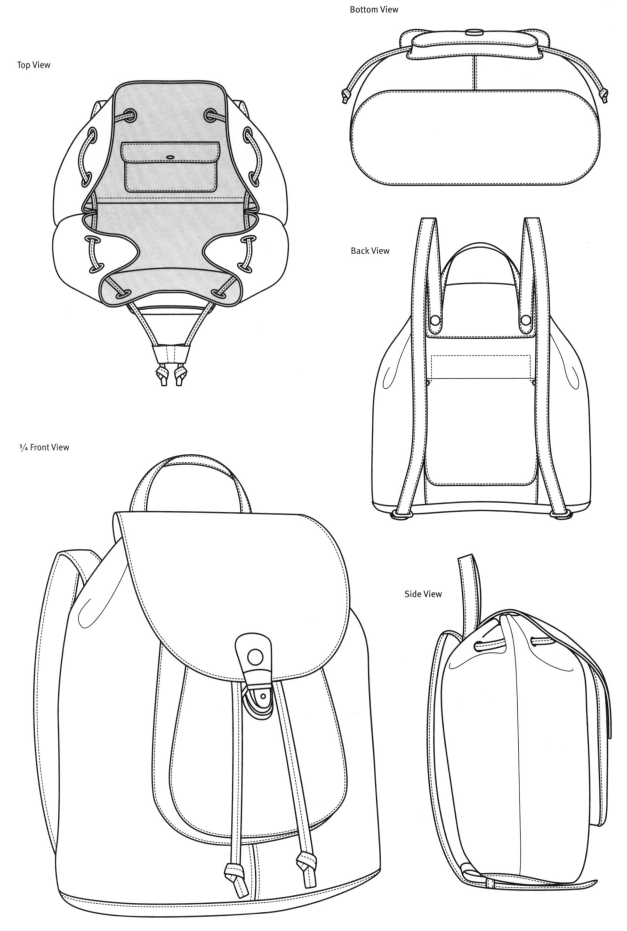

RUCKSACK

"Rucksack" is an alternative name for 'backpack' mainly used in the UK and amongst Western military. The name was borrowed from the German words 'der rücken', which means 'the back of the body', and 'sack', which means 'bag'.

Bottom View

Top View

Back View

¾ Front View

Side View

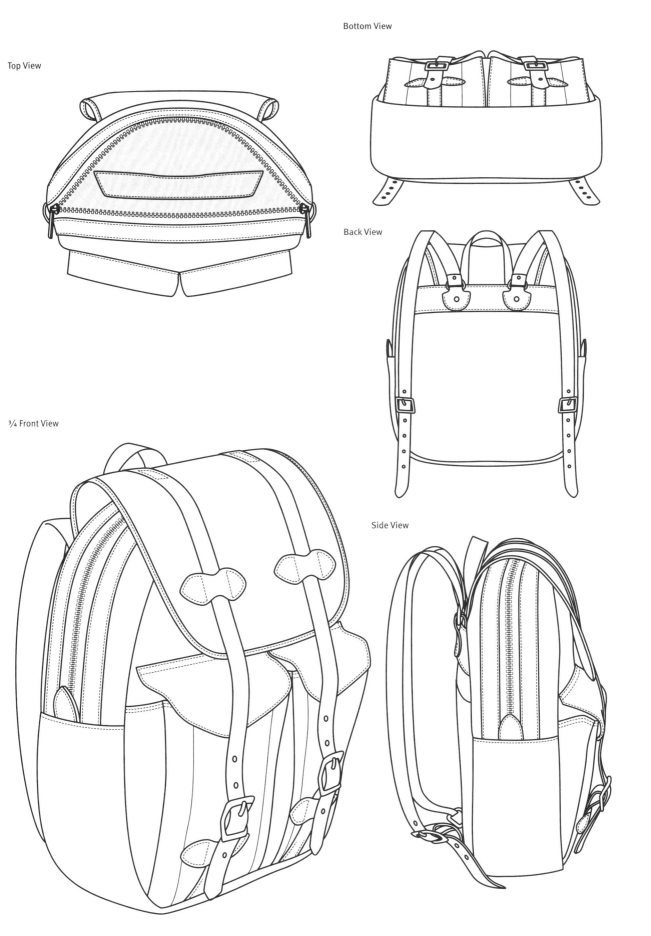

SATCHEL BACKPACK

As its name suggests, it is a backpack with the characteristics of a satchel. It is always made of leather, and features a double-buckled top flap and a front pocket.

Bottom View

Top View

Back View

¾ Front View

Side View

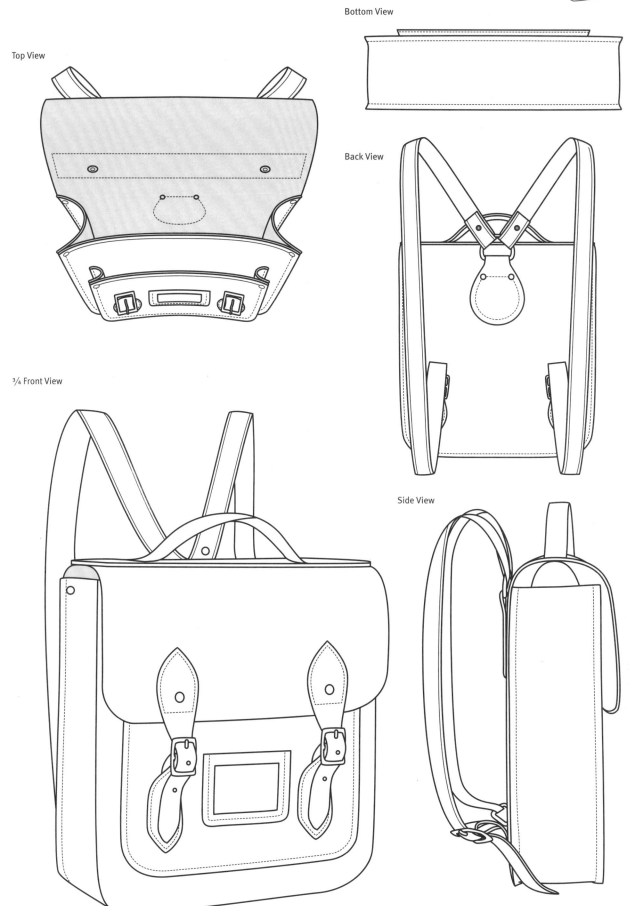

SECURITY POUCH
/ SMALL TRAVELING POUCH

Designed to be worn around the neck and concealed under the clothing, security pouches help safeguard money, documents and other valuables while traveling.

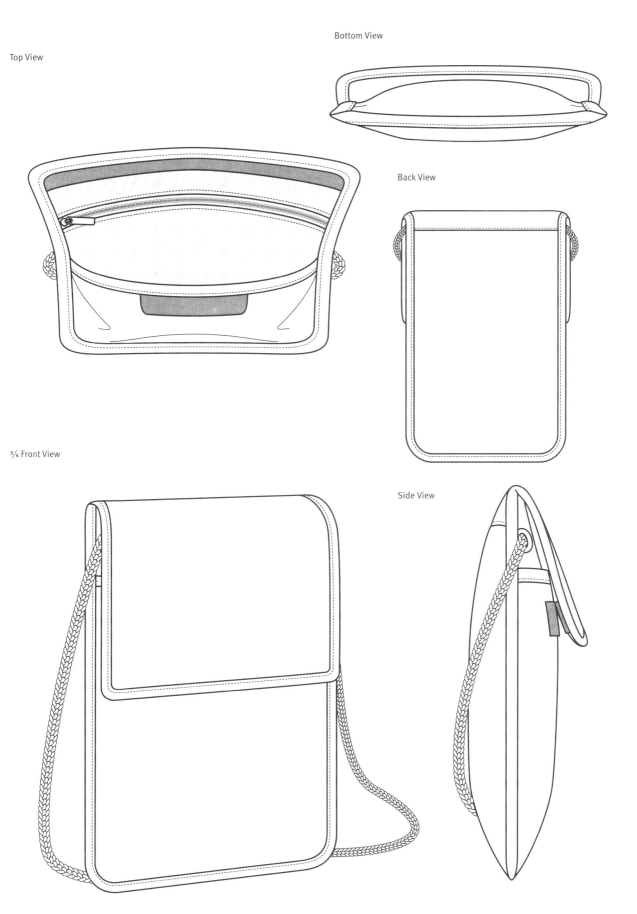

Top View

Bottom View

Back View

¾ Front View

Side View

WASH BAG /
COSMETIC BAG

A small pouch used for holding toiletries and personal grooming items for overnight or longer trips.

Top View

Bottom View

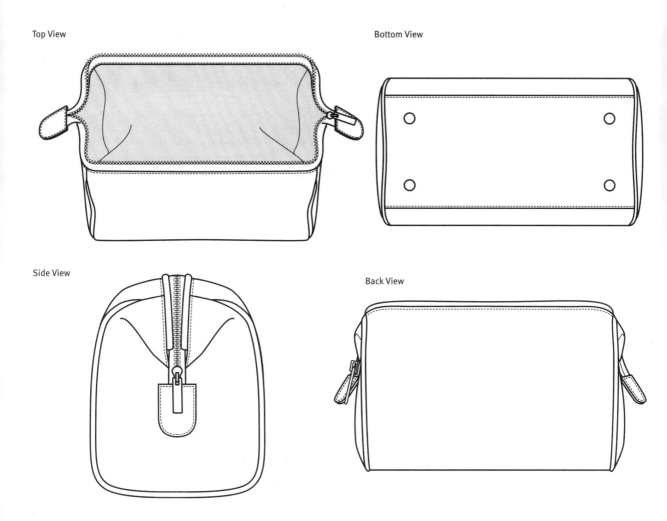

Side View

Back View

¾ Front View

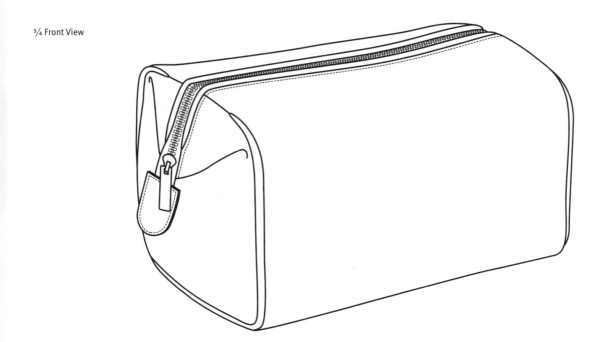

WEEKENDER

Generally with a rectangular base, a weekender is a large leather or fabric bag fastened with a top zipper. It is usually spacious enough to hold personal contents for a short weekend trip.

Bottom View

Top View

Back View

³⁄₄ Front View

Side View

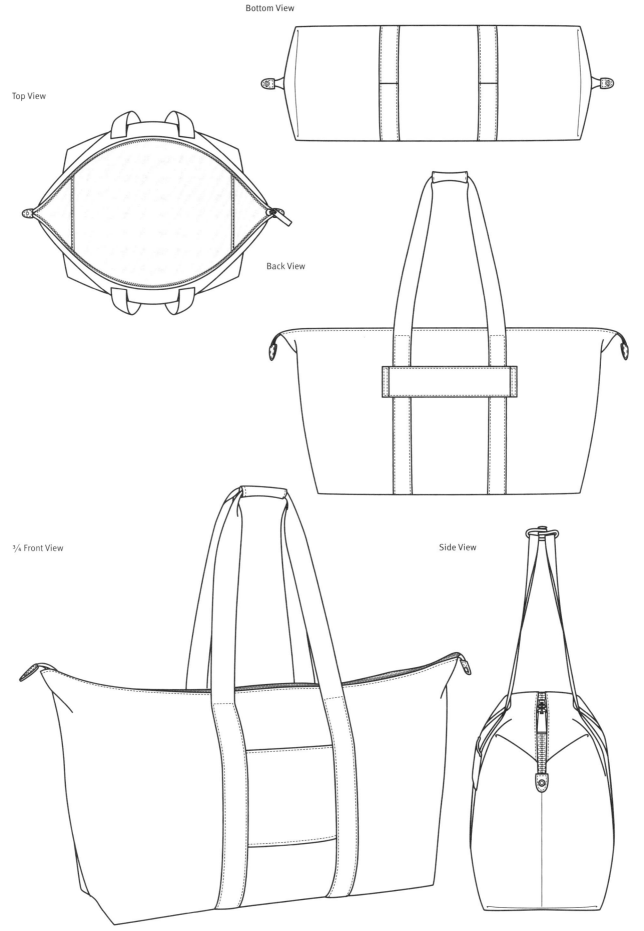

SPORTS DUFFEL BAG

The original 'duffel bag' is characterized by its large size, cylindrical shape and drawstring closure at the top. It is made from a thick cloth which originated from the Belgian town Duffel, from which it got its name. Nowadays, the name broadly applies to any cylindrical shaped bag especially those created for sporting purposes.

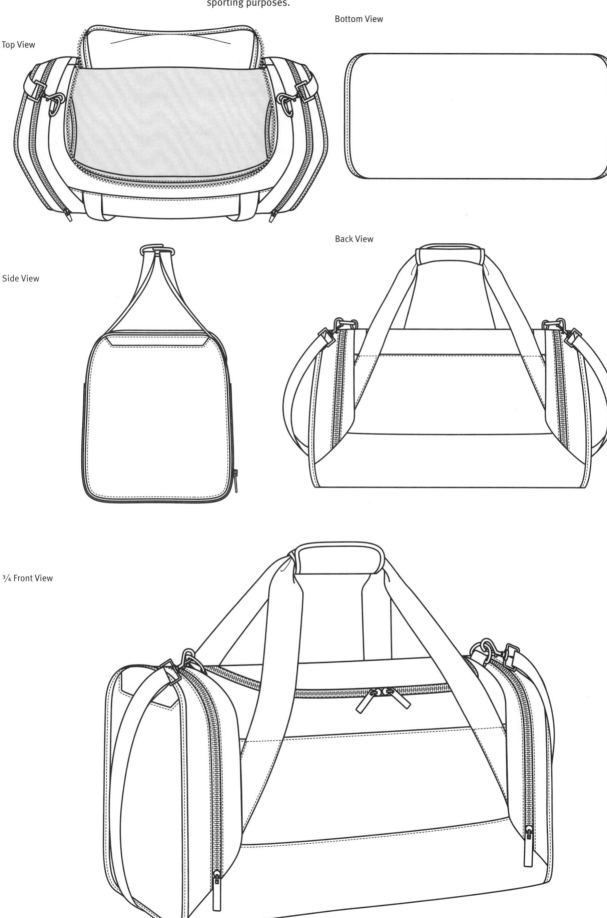

Top View

Bottom View

Side View

Back View

¾ Front View

BARREL BAG
/ HOLDALL

A cylindrical bag with a barrel-shaped compartment. Barrel bags have been popular amongst athletes for decades.

Top View

Bottom View

Side View

Back View

¾ Front View

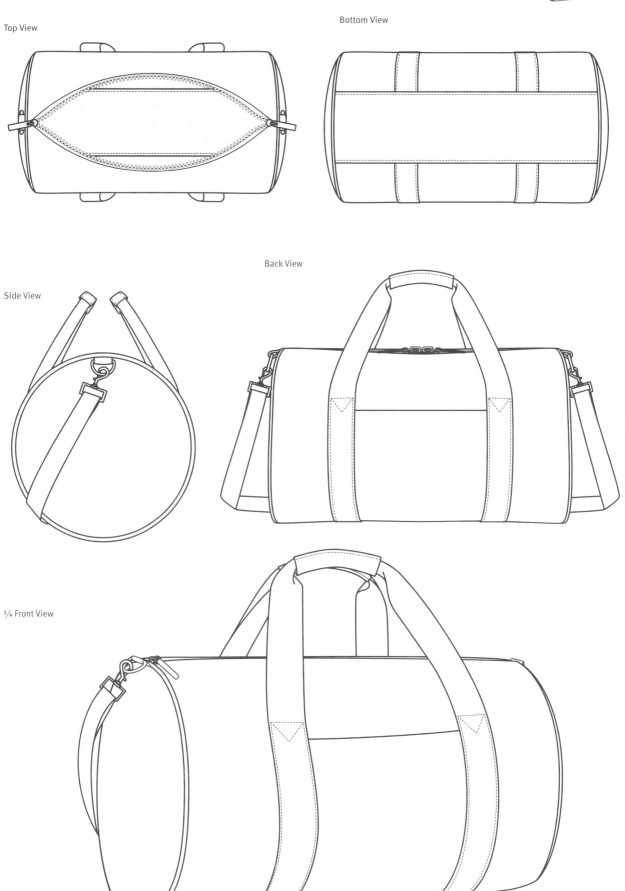

BOWLING BAG

A retro style widely popular in America in the 1990's, the bowling bag was originally designed for carrying bowling balls, bowling shoes and other equipment. It is always trapezium in shape with a wider base, and features two top handles.

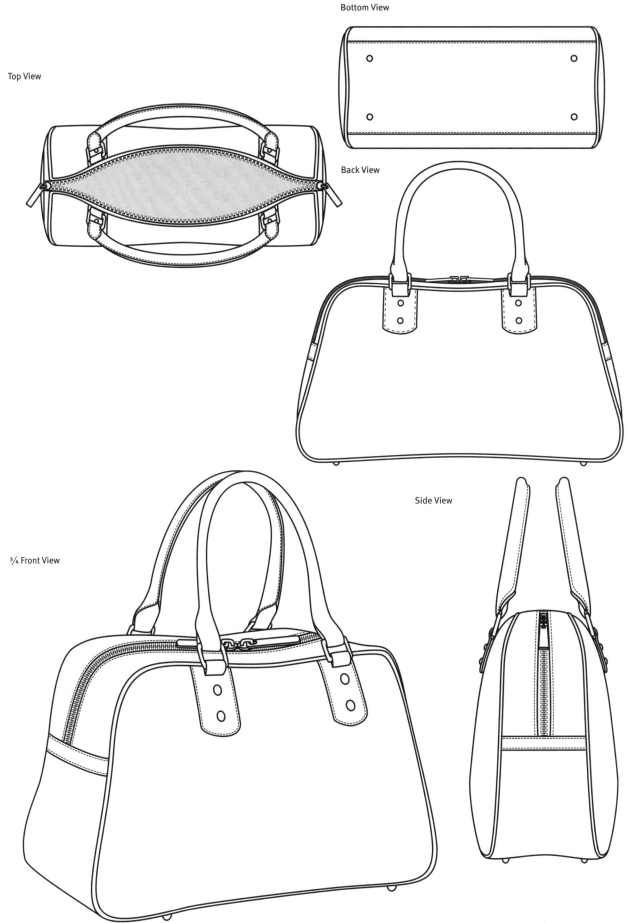

Top View

Bottom View

Back View

¾ Front View

Side View

BOWLING BAG
AS FASHION ITEM

Similar to the original design, modern bowling bags also come in a trapezium shape and feature double top handles, but have dropped the classic piping to create a more streamlined look.

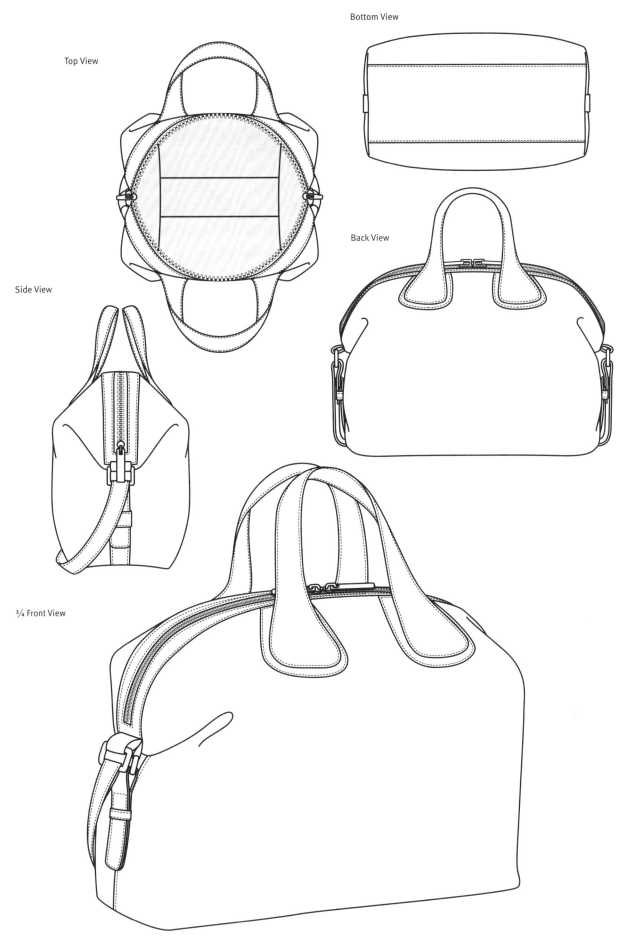

Top View

Bottom View

Side View

Back View

¾ Front View

MESSENGER BAG / COURIER BAG

A large and usually horizontal crossbody bag with a long, adjustable shoulder strap and a flap cover. It is named after the style of bags traditionally carried by mail couriers. The modern-day messenger bag originated from the utility lineman's bag manufactured by De Martini Globe Canvas Company in the 1950's, which was designed for linemen to keep essential gear and tools easily accessible while climbing utility poles.

Top View

Bottom View

Side View

Back View

¾ Front View

FIELD BAG

Designed to withstand long days of fieldwork, field bags are typically made from durable canvas fabrics treated with a water-repellent finish. The style below features a storm flap with two buckled leather straps, and two outer utility pockets.

Top View

Bottom View

Side View

Back View

¼ Front View

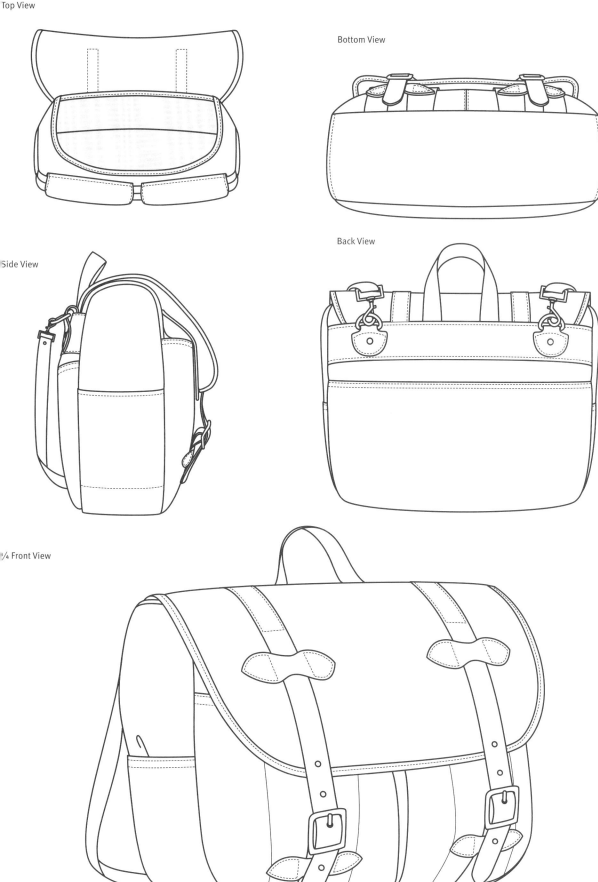

COMPUTER / LAPTOP BAG

A bag designed with padded compartments for holding and protecting a laptop computer.

Top View

Bottom View

Back View

Side View

¾ Front View

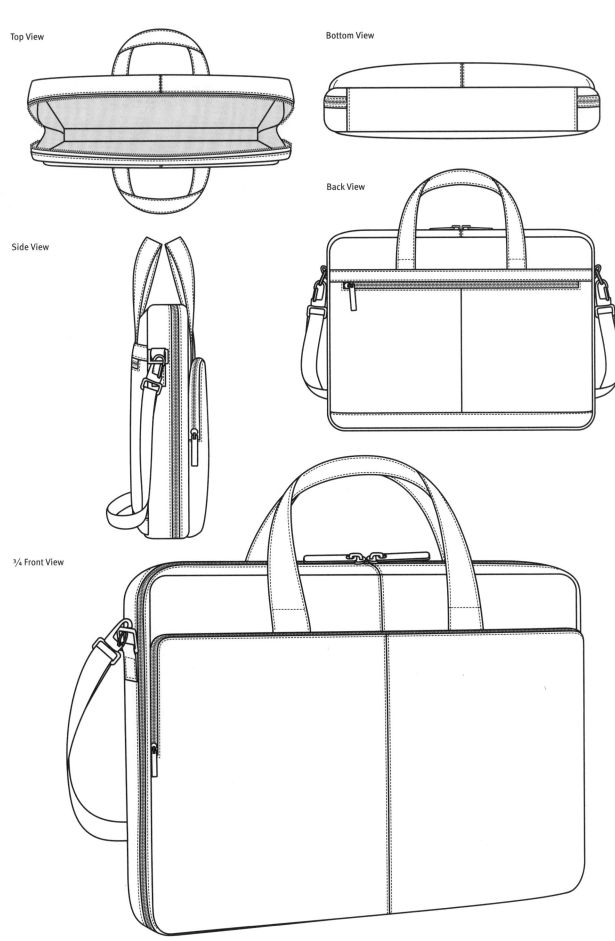

CAMERA BAG

A padded bag with specially designed compartments to hold and protect photography equipment, such as cameras and accessories. Functional camera bags are made from waterproof fabric to protect photography equipment against water and the elements. They should have a molded base to provide stability and stackability.

Top View

Bottom View

Side View

Back View

1/4 Front View

HIKING BACKPACK

Larger sized hiking backpacks are used for longer treks and backcountry trips. An ideal design should have heavily padded shoulder straps and a waist belt. They are more substantial and durable than the regular backpack, and some can sustain up to a couple hundred pounds in weight.

Back View

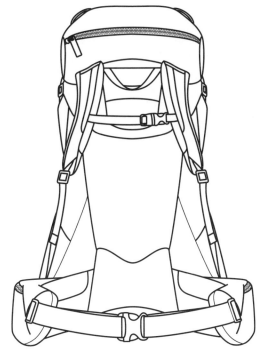

Bottom View

¾ Front View

Side View

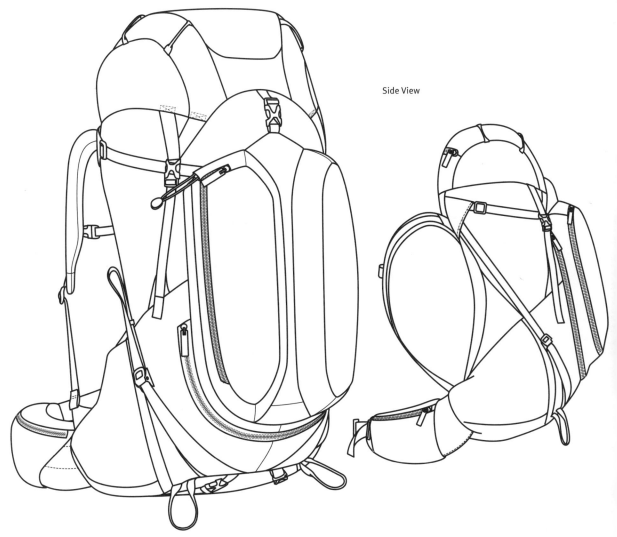

GOLF BAG

A bag designed to hold golfing equipment. It is normally lighter in weight as it is intended to be carried from hole to hole across the golf course. It generally features multiple sections which are separated by rigid support at the top opening. This is to provide better structure and rigidity, as well as for separating golf clubs of different types for easier selection. The side pockets can be used for carrying other equipment and supplies needed over the course of a round of golf.

Top View

Bottom View

Back View

¾ Front View

Side View

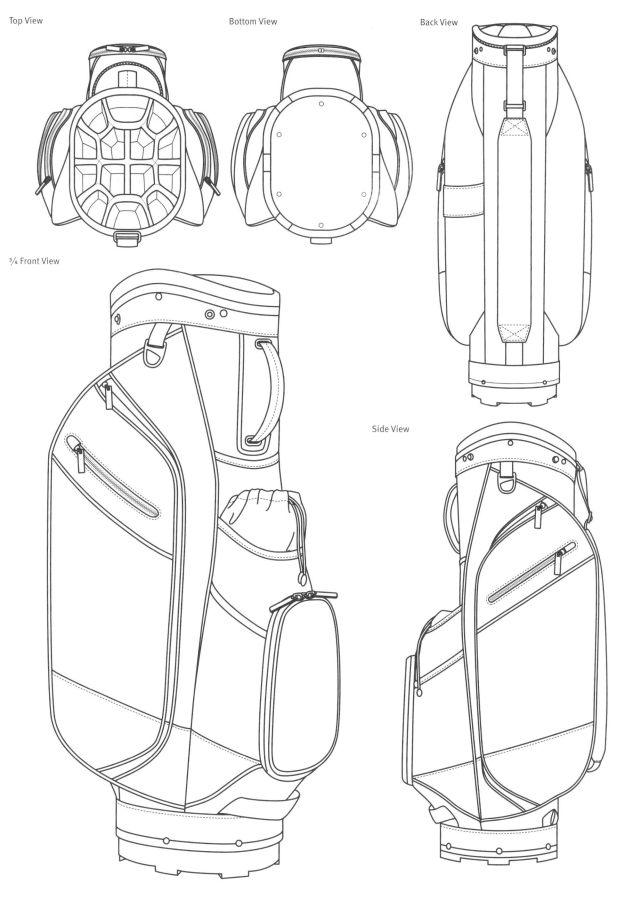

HARDSIDE LUGGAGE

A suitcase constructed from harder and more durable materials, such as aluminum, ABS, polycarbonate, polypropylene, etc. German brand Rimowa is one of the most famous hardside luggage manufacturers in the world. With creating sturdy yet lightweight luggage in mind, Paul Morszeck introduced the first Rimowa suitcase in 1898 – a wooden case which quickly gained popularity amongst worldly travelers. In 1937, his son and successor Richard Morszeck launched the world's first suitcase made of lightweight aircraft aluminum to replace the wooden styles. This Rimova metal suitcase revolutionized the luggage industry and continues to be one of the most iconic and best-selling products of the brand.

¾ Front View

Side View

Bottom View

Back View

Side View

Inside View

SOFTSIDE LUGGAGE
(IN CABIN LUGGAGE SIZE)

Softside luggage is made from more flexible materials such as canvas or nylon, as opposed to the firm and sturdy external structure of hardside suitcases.

Cabin luggage refers to baggage that passengers are allowed to carry with them on-board the passenger compartment of a vehicle or aircraft instead of storing in the cargo compartment. Its size must comply with the cabin restrictions, which may vary from airline to airline.

¾ Front View

Bottom View

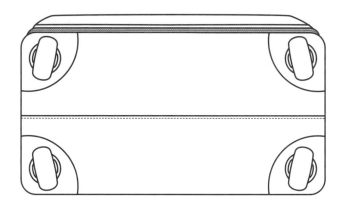

Side View

Back View

Inside View

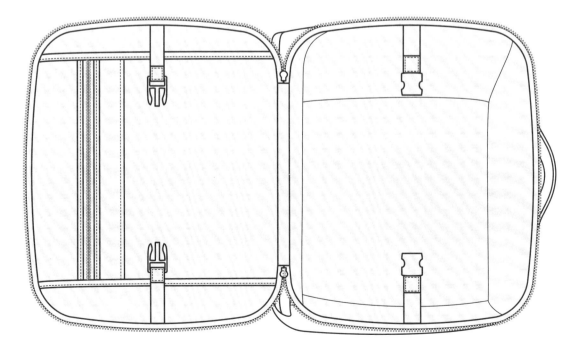

CONTINENTAL / LONG WALLET

A wallet which is longer in shape and can hold banknotes flat and uncreased. Also known as continental wallets, long wallets are fastened by a zipper, leather rein or snap button strap, and commonly feature a coin purse.

Top View

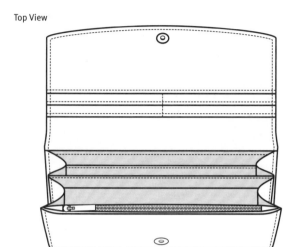

Bottom View

Side View

Back View

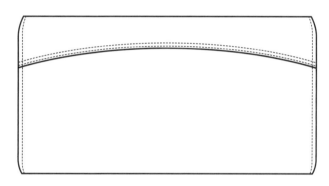

¾ Front View

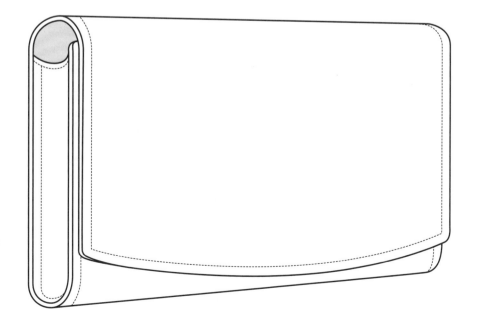

ZIP-AROUND WALLET

A zip-around wallet is one which is fastened by a zipper. It can be either a long, continental sized wallet or a shorter bi-fold sized wallet.

Top View

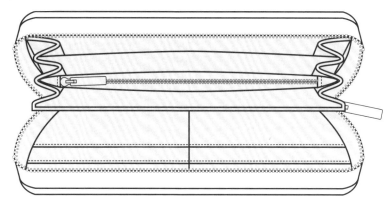

Side View

Bottom View

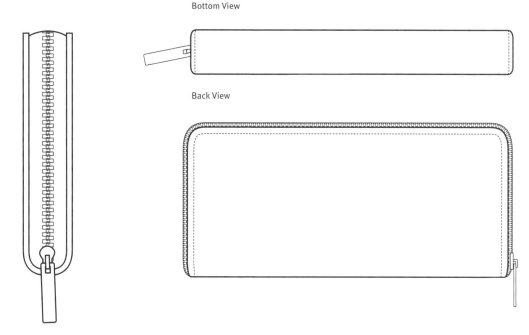

Back View

¾ Front View

BI-FOLD WALLET

A wallet folded into two halves with a center fold. Banknotes are folded over while cards can be stored vertically or horizontally, depending on the design.

Front View

Back View

Inside View

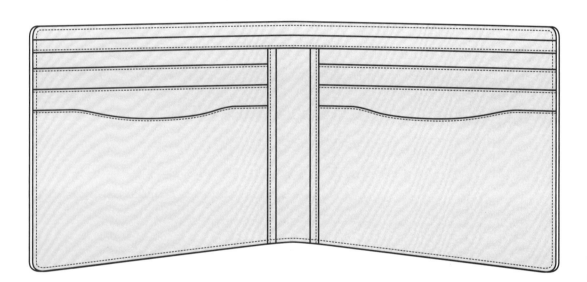

¾ Front View

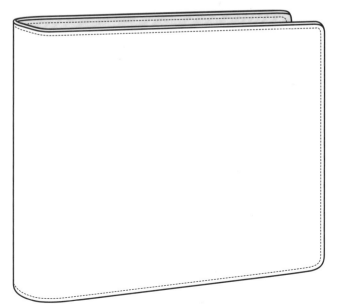

Side View

KEY CASE

Key cases feature hooks or loops to which keys can be attached. Besides key storage, many key cases also serve as multi-functional pocket organizers and may include card slots and smaller pockets. The style below has a snap flap closure, which is a common key case design.

Front View

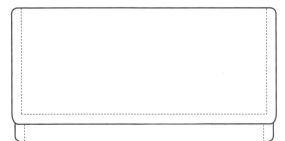

Back View

Inside View

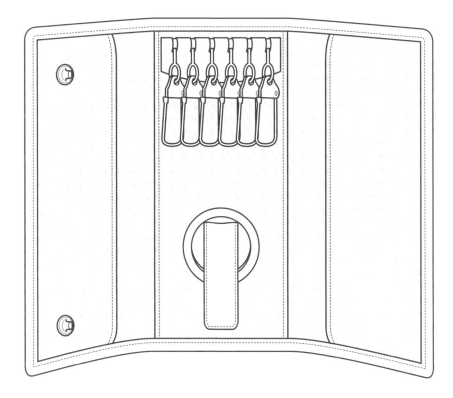

¾ Front View

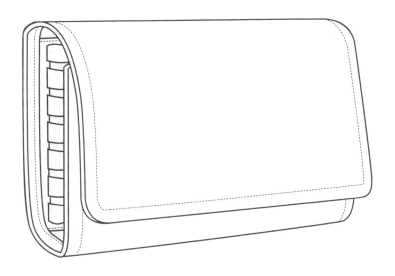

Side View

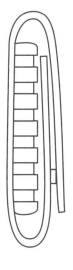

PART VIII

MEASUREMENTS

- COMMON BAG MEASUREMENTS
- SIZE GUIDE FOR BACKPACKS, LUGGAGE AND SMALL LEATHER GOODS
- POCKET SIZE RECOMMENDATION

COMMON BAG MEASUREMENTS

MEASURING A HANDBAG

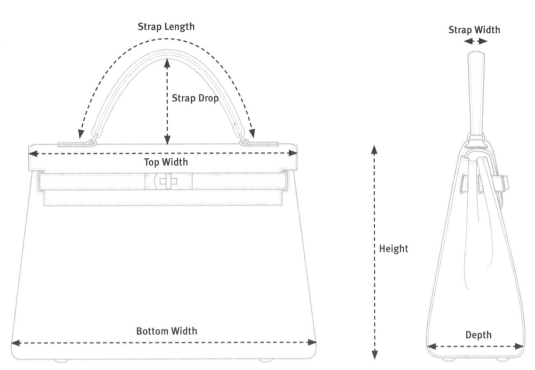

Strap Length	The length of the bag handle / shoulder strap from one end to the other.
Strap Drop	The distance from the base of the strap's highest point to the top center of the bag.
Top Width	The distance between the two furthest points at the top of the bag.
Bottom Width	The distance between the two furthest points at the bottom of the bag.
Height	The measurement from the base to the top center of the bag.
Strap Width	The width of the bag handle / shoulder strap.
Depth	The distance between the two furthest points of the bottom of the bag's side panel.

COMMON SIZE GUIDE FOR BAG STRAP LENGTH AND STRAP DROP

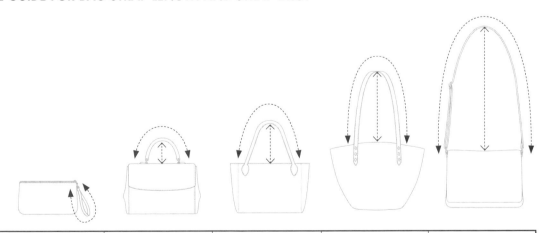

	Wristlet	Top Handle	Shoulder Strap	Long Shoulder Strap	Crossbody Strap
Strap Length	around 30 cm	30 - 45 cm	45 - 66 cm	66 - 101cm	101-127cm
Strap Drop	/	around 18 cm	20 - 30cm	30 - 55cm	≥ 55 cm

SIZE GUIDE FOR BACKPACKS, LUGGAGE AND SMALL LEATHER GOODS

BACKPACK SIZE GUIDE

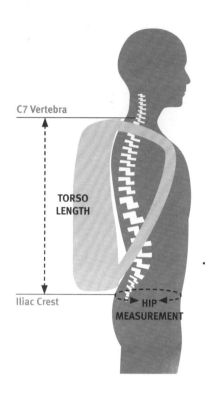

How to measure your torso?
Measure the distance along the curve of the spine, from the base of the neck (i.e. C7 Vertebra) to the center line at the base of the hip (ie. top point of Iliac Crest). This is your torso length.

How to measure your hip?
By using the highest point of the Iliac Crest, measure around this point using a flexible tape. This is your hip measurement.

Backpack Size	Torso Length	Hip Measurement
Extra Small	≤ 40 cm	≤ 55 cm
Small	40 - 44 cm	55 - 69 cm
Medium	45 - 49 cm	70 - 87 cm
Large	50 - 52 cm	88 - 100 cm
Extra Large	≥ 53 cm	≥ 101 cm

CABIN BAGGAGE SIZE GUIDE

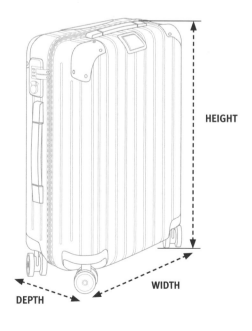

Baggage Size (Height × Width × Depth)	Airline
42 cm × 32 cm × 25 cm	Wizz Air
45 cm × 35 cm × 20 cm	Japan Airlines (domestic flight with less than 100 seats)
48 cm × 36 cm × 20 cm	Aurigny
50 cm × 37 cm × 25 cm	Qatar Airways
50 cm × 40 cm × 25 cm	Etihad Airways
50 cm × 45 cm × 20 cm	Jet Airways (Aircraft Type ATR)
55 cm × 35 cm × 20 cm	Flybe / Blue Islands
55 cm × 35 cm × 25 cm	Air France, Air India, Alitalia, KLM, Jet Airways (Aircraft Type Boeing), Malaysia Airlines
55 cm × 38 cm × 20 cm	Emirates
53 cm × 38 cm × 23 cm	WestJet Airlines
55 cm × 40 cm × 20 cm	Aer Lingus, Aeroflot, Air Berlin, Air China, Asiana Airlines, China Eastern Airlines, Korean Air, Ryanair, Shenzhen Airlines, Sichuan Airlines, Singapore Airlines, TAP Portugal, Thomas Cook Airlines, Thomson Airways, Ukraine International Airlines, Vueling Airlines
55 cm × 40 cm × 23 cm	Air Canada, Austrian Airlines, Edelweiss Air, Lufthansa, Norwegian, Scandinavian Airlines, Swiss International Air Lines, Turkish Airlines
55 cm × 40 cm × 25 cm	All Nippon Airways, Japan Airlines (international flight)
56 cm × 35 cm × 22 cm	JetBlue Airways, United Airlines
56 cm × 35 cm × 23 cm	Delta Air Lines
56 cm × 36 cm × 23 cm	American Airlines, Cathay Pacific Airways, China Airlines, EVA Air, Garuda Indonesia, Vietnam Airlines, Virgin Atlantic
56 cm × 40 cm × 25 cm	Monarch
56 cm × 45 cm × 25 cm	British Airways, EasyJet, Finnair, Iberia, Jet2, Thai Airways International
61 cm × 43 cm × 25 cm	Alaska Airlines

* dimensions include all wheels and handles.

WALLET SIZE GUIDE

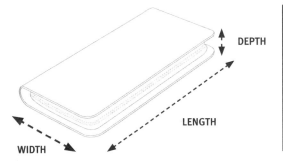

Wallet Size	Dimensions (Length × Width × Depth)	Possible Contents
Small	11 cm × 9 cm × 1.2 cm	notes, credit cards and other cards
Medium	15 cm × 9 cm × 2 cm	notes, coins, credit cards and other cards
Large	19 cm × 10 cm × 3.5 cm	notes, coins, credit cards and other cards, slim mobile phone

BELT SIZE GUIDE

Waist Measurement	Pants Size				Belt Measurement
	US	UK	Euro	Japan	
60 - 70 cm	0 - 2	2 - 6	30 - 34	1 - 5	75 - 85 cm
70 - 80 cm	2 - 6	6 - 10	34 - 38	5 - 9	85 - 95 cm
80 - 90 cm	6 - 10	10 - 14	38 - 42	9 - 13	95 - 105 cm
90 - 100 cm	10 - 14	14 - 18	42 - 46	13 - 17	105 - 115 cm

POCKET SIZE RECOMMENDATION

	For Pens	For Name Cards	For Passport	For Cosmetics	For Sketchbooks	
Pocket Size	14 cm × 3 cm (for 1 pen)	11 cm × 7 cm	14 cm × 11 cm	16 cm × 11 cm	A5	21 cm × 27 cm
					A4	27 cm × 36 cm

	For Mobile Phone		For Tablet		For 11-inch Laptop	For 13-inch Laptop	For 15-inch Laptop
Pocket Size	4.7-inch	16 cm × 9 cm	9.7-inch	24 cm × 18 cm	34 cm × 23 cm	38 cm × 29 cm	42 cm × 31 cm
	5.5-inch	18 cm × 16 cm	12.9-inch	28 cm × 21 cm			